WITHOUT HIM

*A Woman's Guide to Healing and Building a
Relationship with God*

Marissa Ortiz-Cortez

Lincross Publishing

WITHOUT HIM

Cover design by Norbert Elnar
Interior Design by Lance Butler, Concise Consulting Agency
Illustrations by Anquitra Walton & Adesina Walton
ISBN: 978-1-948581-54-7

First Edition: May 2020

This book is dedicated to my grandma, grandpa, mother, godmother, stepdad, a loving family, and friends. Thank you to all those who have prayed over me and asked God for my healing.

CONTENTS

INTRODUCTION

I started writing this book in the middle of a difficult time in my life. It was during this season of my life that my childhood pain, insecurities, and feelings of inadequacy came to the surface. I was also in an unhealthy relationship and I was plummeting into self-destruction. I was drinking, stealing, using drugs, entertaining unhealthy friendships, and dating the wrong men. The only time I talked to God was when I was at rock bottom emotionally: "God if you just get me out of this situation, I'll stop..." only to return to my self-destructive behaviors once God pulled me out of the situation. My only knowledge of God or religion was the distant God my grandmother told me to whisper prayers to as a child. I only went to church for funerals and weddings. That was all I knew about God.

It wasn't until I was completely broken emotionally that I became desperate for inner healing and that is how I found God. I was binge drinking and combining different drugs in a single night. There were times I thought I would die in the middle of the night while I was asleep because of how many drugs I had taken. I was stealing from local stores just to feel a rush of excitement in my life. I had this disregard for my own life, and it began to scare me.

I first began to seek God in small ways. I would pray while drunk in the restrooms of bars or I'd ask God to keep me alive throughout the night while on drugs. I took a bigger step closer to God when I started going to a local church near my apartment. I began to ask God to heal my heart while sitting in churches alone. I would sit alone and just talk to Jesus. While searching for knowledge about God I learned that He sent Jesus, His only son to die on the cross for our sins so that our souls could be saved. He sent Jesus so that we could live with joy and peace.

Jesus answered, "I am the way and the truth and the life. No one comes to the Father except through me. If you really know me, you will know my Father as well. From now on, you do know Him and have seen Him."

John 14:6-7

When I started seeking God for myself, I started to build a relationship with God and not religion. Religion had taught me I was unworthy of the God everyone spoke about, so I was discouraged from seeking any real relationship with Him. One reason why some of us can't begin to start a relationship with Jesus is that we've been hurt by others or we've hurt ourselves. Some of us may have a misconception about God because we have used the beliefs of society and others to form our opinion of Jesus without getting to know Him ourselves.

Before sitting in those churches, I had this misconception that I could never satisfy the God that people spoke about. So, I continued living my life with no accountability because I thought I could never live up to God's standards so why try. That mindset led to my brokenness and absolute self-destruction. I encourage you to seek Jesus for yourself and build your own relationship with Him.

In this book, I hope to deconstruct the idea that we need to be perfect to start a relationship with God. Even if we've made mistakes in the past it doesn't mean that God doesn't love us anymore. It also doesn't mean that we are banned from ever starting a relationship with Him. We have never known a love like God's love. He loves us so much and He forgives us. His love is so beautiful and powerful it transforms our hearts and minds. You will learn that as you start to build a relationship with Him. Building a relationship with God is a process and I want to normalize that you will still make mistakes when you're walking with Jesus because you're human. God knows we're human and He knows we will make mistakes but don't let that discourage you from seeking a life with Him. To have a human experience here on earth means that we will make mistakes, but God will forgive us if we dare to be honest with Him about all of our mistakes. God doesn't demand us to be perfect to start a relationship with Him, He just wants us to start where we are. So, the good news is that if you've made many mistakes like I have, God will still welcome you with an embrace.

Once I built a relationship with God, I was able to develop into the woman I am today. My inner world and outer world began to transform. New friendships, relationships, career opportunities began to manifest in my life. I would be lying if I said it was easy because there was a season that God had to remove old friendships and relationships that no longer served who God was calling me to be and that was difficult. The Lord even removed some familiar coping mechanisms, destructive habits, thoughts, and behaviors and that was also difficult to let go of.

Although I lost much, I gained much. God restored my life with even greater things like a relationship with Him, self-love, peace, and joy. He gave me a new life.

While I'm not perfect nor do I claim to be perfect. I do strive to be the best version of myself spiritually, mentally, and intellectually. When I started this journey with Jesus I was completely broken: I was drinking, stealing, dating recklessly, and in a toxic group of friends but after walking with God, my life transformed into something so beautiful. My life continues to have so much beauty with Jesus in it. I've learned to navigate the storms that life will bring and I've learned to enjoy the beauty of small moments. If you already have a relationship with Jesus but still feel enslaved to your past, this book is also for you. I had been walking with the Lord for some time but still, for a long time I was enslaved to my childhood insecurities and past heartaches. When I started to chase after God's heart, I was able to let go of superficial attempts to fill my emptiness. The Lord revealed in prayer that I was seeking a career, men, and my beauty for worth and validation. I was drinking to run from my heartache and childhood. But what God had to offer was way better than alcohol, drugs, and spending time with people who didn't care about my well-being. God has proved his love to me every day since I started my journey with Him. When you start your journey with Him, He will reveal the same to you.

I'm so thankful that God pulled me away from my past when He did because now, I am writing this book. Throughout my journey, I have seen God touch the lives of others when they were at rock bottom and that is exactly how it happened for me. I have found a path that has healed my heart from insecurity, childhood trauma, and heartbreak. It didn't happen overnight, but it did happen. I am not perfect, and I still have moments when I don't have everything together, but I have come a long way from crying out to God on floors wondering if I would ever be healed. This book is for the woman wondering if she is beautiful enough, smart enough, or worthy enough. This is for the woman always searching for a relationship or external validation to feel worthy. This is for the woman still experiencing rage from childhood abandonment and disappointments. I want you to know that with Jesus you can feel whole and you will get over that heartbreak. I don't claim to have all the answers, but I have been heartbroken by the people I have loved most and healed. I am a woman that has learned my worth and purpose by building a relationship with God. If you find something in this book that makes you feel stronger, heals you, enlightens you, carry it with you; I pray that God heals every area of your life and releases you from the bondage of your past. To start a relationship with God we just have to start where we are and take one step at a time, leaving the past versions of ourselves behind and embracing the woman that God created us to be. With this book, I hope you learn that you never have to live without God and He can heal all parts of you.

When Jesus spoke again to the people, He said, "I am the light of the world. Whoever follows me will never walk in darkness but will have the light of life."

John 8:12

CHAPTER ONE

CHILDHOOD WOUNDS

I believe understanding the emotional childhood wounds of a person is a key to understanding a person's behaviors, thoughts, and belief system. It is difficult to deal with childhood emotional wounds caused by abuse, rejection, abandonment, disappointment, betrayal, and judgment. Usually, emotional wounds are inflicted by those closest to us and often emotional wounds aren't necessarily our fault but we're left to deal with the pain of them anyway. Emotional wounds that occur in childhood affect our overall sense of worth, identity, and future relationships if we don't heal them.

It wasn't until I started my walk with the Lord that I was able to heal the emotional wounds from my past. As I became closer with Jesus, He opened the door to my past so I could see how my past was affecting my present. It will be difficult to face your past because most of us have repressed painful experiences to carry on with our lives. We call that healing but that is only masking the pain to the best of our human ability. Pain that is only masked or hidden from our consciousness will not heal on a deeper level. Jesus is the only one that can heal our pain on the deepest level so it no longer negatively affects us. Under no circumstances did I want to confront my childhood because I believed coping was easier if I simply forgot all the disappointment and hurt. I thought if I just locked it away somewhere in the back of my heart that it couldn't hurt me anymore but that wasn't the case.

If a memory still has the power to invoke a strong emotional response from you when you think about it, the enemy has an open door to your mind. The enemy of our soul, the devil wants to keep us chained to our hurtful past so we'll stay stuck in depression, fear, shame, regret, and disappointment. If you experience grief, regret, shame, sadness, when you think about a particular memory the enemy can use that for his benefit. You don't want to give the enemy or your past, power over you. I could tell my past was still affecting me because I couldn't bring myself to trust or love people. I would think of those in my childhood who had hurt me, and the enemy would remind me as an adult that I couldn't trust those around me. The enemy wants access to our lives and what better way than through our mind, thoughts, and memories. For those of us who were hurt during our childhood, the enemy hoped to use our past to keep us emotionally stagnant but with Jesus, we can break free from his grip over our minds.

I want to tell you that it is possible to let go of your painful childhood because Jesus can and He will break the chains that the enemy has placed on your life. Healing an aspect of your identity that is so rooted in your soul is difficult to heal on your own but it's not difficult for God. If you want to know why you can't trust others or why you can't love without being afraid, ask God. I had to go back to the beginning and find out what exactly it was about my childhood that was causing my mistrust in others and my mistrust in God. In this chapter, I want you to begin to challenge yourself to uncover painful parts of your childhood. I want you to ask yourself what experiences from your childhood are still affecting you and bring them to Jesus.

As I began to sit with God during prayer, memories began to flow into my mind. The most significant memory God brought to my mind was the death of my father. When I was seven, my father died and afterward my mother struggled with her demons. I remember looking at my father's casket wondering if he'd ever wake up because I was too young to grasp the concept of human death. I know very little about my father, only the stories that I've been told by those who knew him well and I've been told he adored me, his only child. I have asked God to give me peace about my father's death and He has.

After my father died everything changed and the following months were difficult for my mother and I. We both laid in her room during the day with dark curtains blocking out sunlight. I remember those moments vividly. There were times I'd leave her room to play in the living room alone and other times I'd stay in bed with her in the dark. After some time, it was decided that I should live with my grandmother for a period of time. I certainly missed my mother and needed her to make sense of the sudden changes in my life. I'm grateful that my grandparents and godmother were able to support and nurture me during this time. Still, at seven years old I began to deal with a sense of perceived abandonment and rejection. Those spirits of rejection and abandonment have trailed behind me my entire life—affecting my self-esteem, relationships, and decisions. The enemy has used events in my childhood to keep me enslaved to the fear of abandonment for years.

It's important to examine our childhood wounds because they can explain our belief systems and our patterns in relationships. Since I watched my mother endure such a hardship in my childhood, I developed a caretaker complex and I felt it was my responsibility to take care of others emotionally at the expense of my well-being and peace. Every time I got into a new relationship, I felt an obligation to emotionally caretake for partners which led me into a lot of unhealthy relationships and friendships which I will elaborate in later chapters.

I also began to feel as though I was a burden on those around me because others were given the responsibility to support me as a child. I felt a sense of unworthiness and I remember feeling humiliated because I felt pity from others because of my circumstances, and I resented it. My deeply rooted shame began to take on another form as I grew into an adult. It was challenging for me to receive help from others and I started to strive up the ladder of success to prove that I was worthy according to society's standards. I became very prideful, head-strong, and I wanted to be perfect in all areas of life. When I fell short of perfection, I criticize myself harshly for not being good enough. I had an "I can do it" attitude and I refused to be vulnerable with others because it brought up my childhood when I had to depend on others for support and love.

Since childhood, I have experienced the crippling fear of abandonment, unworthiness, and rejection. Those dark spirits have affected every friendship and relationship I've ever had. I say spirits because there are dark spirits that want power over our minds and lives. If we believe in angels and God then we must face the fact that there are also dark entities in the spiritual realm that want access to our hearts, soul, and thoughts. If dark spirits can keep us chained to fear, hate, depression, they win dominion over all areas of our lives. However, with the power of God and angels, we have the power to overcome our past and our negative feelings.

Childhood memories are so powerful because they leave a scar on our hearts. We fear to love, fear to trust, and fear to be disappointed because our caretakers hurt us. It's important to take an honest inventory of your heart so you can track your first emotional wounds. It will be difficult to feel all those feelings that we've tried so hard to forget but if we can bring them to surface, God can start to heal them.

I was tired of replaying the same story over and over in my mind about my childhood and I was tired of being the victim in my story. When I took ownership of my past and invited God to heal it, I was set free from being a slave to my past. And what used to be my crippling pain is now my power to heal others. Don't entertain the enemy and sulk in the grief of your past. Decide that you want more for yourself. Decide that you want peace. Whenever I felt the enemy bring up my past, I would remind myself that Jesus died on the cross so that I could live a life filled with peace. Don't let your childhood hold you back from the life that God wants you to have.

Our past is valuable because it explains our habits, beliefs, and why we respond the way we do. I don't want to dismiss any of your painful experiences or memories because they're meaningful. I understand what it feels like to be hurt and I don't want to invalidate your feelings because your feelings are valid. So, I won't say the past doesn't matter but I don't want the enemy to keep using your past to keep you chained to depression, anxiety, and fear. Asking God to heal those childhood pains requires letting God walk you through the storms of your past and trusting that with all His power you will be healed on the other side and that you will finally forgive those who have disappointed you. If a dark memory arises again simply say "I gave that hurtful memory to God" and carry on with your day. Don't let the enemy continue to take your mind to dark places or the wilderness after God has set you free. We must do our part to seek God for healing and fight the good fight of faith. We can do that by reading the Bible and trusting that God will ease your pain regarding your past. This scripture below perfectly demonstrates how we must also want our inner healing while asking God to deliver us.

Inside these porches lay many sick people. Some were blind. Some could not walk. Some could not move their bodies. An angel of the Lord came at certain times and made the water move. All of them were waiting for it to move. Whoever got in the water first after it was moving was healed of whatever sickness he had.
A man was there who had been sick for **thirty-eight years**. Jesus saw him lying there and knew the man had been sick a long time. Jesus said to him, **"Would you like to be healed?"** The sick man said, "Sir, I have no one to put me in the pool when the water is moving. While I am coming, another one gets in first." **Jesus said to him, "Get up! Pick up your bed and walk." At once the man was healed and picked up his bed and walked.**
This happened on the Day of Rest.
John 5:3-9

The man in the scripture had been lying by the pool waiting for his chance to be healed by the healing properties of the water. For thirty-eight years this man waited and watched as others got their healing. When Jesus came. He asked the man, "Would you like to be healed?" The man replied, "Sir I have no one to put me in the pool." No human being is going to do all the work for us. We must get up, pick up our bed, and walk forward. We must continuously seek God through prayer and reading the Bible to find healing. So, I ask you. Do you want to get well? Do you want to heal? Do you want to let go of your past? If the answer is yes, continue to seek the Lord because you will find healing.

While I was healing, I used a journal to write my prayers and track my healing. Every day the length of prayers varied; sometimes it was a few sentences and sometimes a few paragraphs. As I began to write my hurtful memories I came face to face with my wounded soul and heart.

I want you to start a journal while you're reading this book and begin to write your prayers and feelings. Use the journal as a way to be vulnerable with God. You can ask angels to protect you from any dark spirits or ask Jesus for anything. You can also just thank Him and give Him praise. For this chapter, I want you to take a moment to write down the memories or events that have hurt you the most and see if they are still hurting you today. If they are, courageously invite God into those areas of your life.

I promise that God wants to heal painful experiences for you and He will. Just know that even though we can petition God and He will answer our prayers, it will be on His timing. I know this from personal experience because there were times that I would pray and the next morning I felt a strong sense of relief and clarity. I would get up to go to work and I could feel the pain from the previous night lifted off my chest. In contrast, I have spent nights in tears praying for God to help me with something and it would take more than just a night to see God answer my prayer. Those were the times I had to consistently seek God to help me because the hurtful memories of my past would keep coming up again and again. This may sound discouraging because we want God to answer immediately, but it was those times that the Lord didn't answer my prayers immediately that made me more grounded in my faith. I had to seek Him multiple times and show Him that no matter how long it took I wasn't going to give up on seeking Him. I was going to trust that He was going to walk me through the storm. Each time I went to pray and fight the spiritual battle, the pain would diminish a little until it was eventually gone. While believing in God for the healing of my childhood I came across this scripture.

And Jesus said, "Who was it that touched me?" When all denied it, Peter said, "Master, the crowds surround you and are pressing in on you!" **But Jesus said, "Someone touched me, for I perceive that power has gone out from me."** And when the woman saw that she was not hidden, she came trembling and falling down before him declared in the presence of all the people why she had touched him, and **how she had been immediately healed.** And he said to her, **"Daughter, your faith has made you well; go in peace. Luke 8:45-48**

I noticed the power of prayer when I could sit with those childhood memories and they would no longer affect me the way they once did. Memories of my mother were the hardest because they would cause me pain, anger, and shame. Although she has been incredibly supportive in my adulthood, I believe the enemy wanted me to hold on to the past so my anger could burn. I began to pray to the Lord to help me discipline my mind to let go of these hurtful memories and forgive. I developed a strong prayer life during this time because I was trusting God to help me let go of my past. It took awhile for me to see my prayers be answered but when I started to heal, I began to see that season of unanswered prayers through a different lens. I was no longer seeing it through the lens of pain but through the lens of God's wisdom.

But he said to me, "My grace is sufficient for you, for my power is made perfect in weakness." Therefore, I will boast all the more gladly about my weaknesses, so that Christ's power may rest on me.

2 Corinthians 12:9

We become wiser and stronger when God doesn't answer our prayers right away. It allows us to press into God when we're trusting Him. Those who love God will not be disappointed in the grand scale of things. Don't be discouraged if the healing doesn't happen immediately, I know my God well enough to know that if He isn't answering a prayer right away there's a purpose in your season of waiting. You must make sure to be diligent and remind yourself that even if God isn't healing the issue you have at this exact moment it doesn't mean that He won't. Continue to fight the fight of faith and keep seeking God for healing. When God didn't answer my prayer, I saw Him use the difficult memories to strengthen my ability to rely on Him and trust that He would help me forgive.

Now, I'm able to speak about the memories and use them for God's glory. The incidents that I once could not even acknowledge in my mind I'm able to use to help someone else heal and learn to put their trust in God. The length of time it takes to heal will vary differently for everyone, but God will do it if you put all your faith in Him.

Besides asking God to heal my childhood I needed to change how I saw God. I needed to see God as a loving Father. I had this false belief that the God I whispered prayers to as a child had ignored me. I believed God had abandoned me. God is not going to let you down the way the people in your past have. He will bring you the people you need to grow.

As I reflect, I can tell you that God was truly there guiding each one of my steps. He had sent angels to protect me along the way and people to support me throughout my life. My nina, grandparents, friends, coaches, and teachers cared deeply about me. They nurtured me and protected me while I was developing and growing. It is because of the people God placed in my life that led to my beautiful growth.

Coach Joe, a man who became an influential male figure in my life would pick me up for practices and games when I played softball in middle school. I was starting to rebel against my mom and hanging around the wrong crowd. Coach Joe always believed in me more than I believed in myself. He taught me discipline, hard work, and perseverance. He taught me crucial lessons that I'm able to carry with me now. He taught me that even when our team was losing, the game wasn't over until the last inning. Even if we had lost the entire game with hard work we could still win even in the last inning. He taught me the importance of working towards a goal. Now I incorporate that lesson into my relationship with God. No matter how far we fall away from God we can get back up and still have a relationship with God. With God, we get to start over and redeem our mistakes. Even if we've made mistake after mistake the game isn't over.

When you look back towards the hard times in your life, think of those who were there to support you and encourage you and you'll find the small lessons and blessings that each person has brought to your life. God knows exactly who we need in our lives. He also knows exactly who to remove if a person has the potential to harm us. The key is to learn to trust who He brings and who He takes out of our lives.

Although I had spent my childhood feeling rejected, I now use my life to remind women that they will never be rejected by God. Even my heartbreaks were instrumental in molding the woman that I've become and for the first time in my life I can truly say that I'm happy with who I am and I'm excited. Each rejection, disappointment, and heartache has led me to the woman I am now.

The purpose of the devil is to kill, steal, and destroy. He wants to destroy your purpose, steal your joy, keep you from love, and defeat your mind. Some of us are wounded so badly in our past that we live the rest of our lives only half alive walking around with agony in our hearts. Our capacity to love, heal, and help others is a threat to the devil so he keeps us in a state of sadness and defeat. He doesn't want to see you experience God's love so you can stay stuck in your past, never moving forward. Don't let the enemy use your past to keep you unhappy and stagnant any longer. The Lord wants you to be joyful and experience the beauty life has to offer. The devil and dark spirits work to keep us in the dark, in depression and fear.

If your parent or caretaker has hurt you in some way during your childhood, allow God to heal those emotional wounds from your past so you can embrace the life God wants you to have. God doesn't want us to carry the pain of our past into our future. The enemy uses our brokenness and painful past to keep us bonded to our pain and our fears. If we're paralyzed with fear and feelings of unworthiness our soul won't move forward and the enemy wins. If the enemy wins we won't seek God and we won't know true love because we're complacent with being chained to our pain. It may be hard to forgive those who have hurt you but God will help you. God's love is pure and even if family has hurt you, God can restore you and anything you've lost. If you simply can't reconcile with family who has hurt you because it's not safe physically or emotionally, know that you are God's family and He will supply you with the love and people you need. The closer we get to God the more we will experience unconditional love and take the necessary healing steps away from our painful childhoods.

Scripture to Meditate

Even if my father and mother abandoned me, the LORD cares for me.
Psalm 27:10

Can a woman forget her nursing child, that she should have no compassion on the son of her womb? Even these may forget, yet I will not forget you
Isaiah 49:15

It is the Lord who goes before you. He will be with you; he will not leave you or forsake you. Do not fear or be dismayed.
Deuteronomy 31:8

I will make My dwelling among you, and My soul will not reject nor separate itself from you.
I will walk among you and be your God, and you shall be My people.
Leviticus 26:11-12

The Lord is near to the brokenhearted and saves the crushed in spirit.
Psalm 34:18

Prayer

Lord, I pray you heal the memories of my past. I have held onto the dark moments of my childhood for far too long. I want to move forward. Please come and heal my heart. Renew my mind and help me to embrace the new life that you have for me. I want to be healed so help me to forgive those who have hurt me just as you have forgiven me. In Jesus' name, amen.

CHAPTER TWO

OUR BAD CHOICES CAN BE MADE BEAUTIFUL WITH GOD

Some of us have made so many mistakes in life that we feel we can't redeem ourselves. We do a considerable amount of damage in our lives and fall into self-destruction until we hit rock bottom. We stay in darkness and continue to make bad choices because we believe we're beyond saving anyway. The hard thing about personal bad choices is that we must take ownership of them and we can't blame others. Many of us have found it easier to blame others for our misfortune but blaming others solves nothing. Luckily, even our bad decisions can be redeemed by God. He can take the broken parts of our lives and transform them into something beautiful. I want to encourage you to begin taking steps toward forgiving yourself for your past choices and start moving forward.

Our mistakes don't mean that we can't fix or build a relationship with God. We absolutely can have a relationship with God despite our mistakes and He will change the outcome of our lives. That is why God sent Jesus to earth. Jesus died on the cross for our mistakes and He has redeemed us. The way we mend our connection to God is seeking Jesus. Through Jesus, we can experience all God has to offer in life which is forgiveness, love, peace, and happiness.

God is the creator of everything and He can transform every past mistake so why not let Him. He can help you move past the most difficult experiences and regrets, all you have to do is give him your heart. While that may sound frightening because some of us have given our hearts to others and have been disappointed. That is the beautiful thing about God, He has the power to change your story at any moment. Unfortunately, some of us become so filled with shame and embarrassment that we can't come to God to admit our mistakes. The enemy convinces us that there is no redemption for us but that isn't true. Jesus takes our mistakes, heals them, and helps us move past them.

There have been times I felt I was beyond saving because I kept making the same mistakes. However, through those mistakes, I learned that God was very forgiving. I personally struggled with drugs and alcohol in high school and college. Two years before I went off to college I was a mess and I struggled with making bad decisions. I was ditching school to drink or use drugs with friends. My grades weren't important to me and I picked up a habit of stealing.

Just as my life was on a downward spiral, God intervened. In my junior year of high school, I moved schools away from my old friends who I used drugs with. My best friend Alyssa was at this new school and she was just the friend that I needed in that particular season in my life. As I reflect toward that moment, I can see how intentional God was with our friendship. That's one of the beautiful things about God is that He brings just the right people into our lives to push us to be the best versions of ourselves. She was a fierce friend and she challenged me to be better academically.

God always has a way of pulling us out of certain environments when we are destined for something greater. If you're being put into a new position, school, or city trust that the Lord has something better in mind for you. If He takes you out of a certain environment, trust that He knows where to place you so that you'll flourish beautifully. God knows what we need for our next step, learn to trust Him with your life.

At this new school, I managed to pass all my courses and make-up failed classes from the years before. A voice in me urged me to make up for my mistakes. Now I understand that voice was the Holy Spirit. I had done a considerable amount of damage, so I had to work harder than anyone else if I wanted to graduate. I went to night school that ended at 7 p.m. and I woke up earlier than my classmates to attend a 6 a.m. class to make up courses I had failed at my previous school. I stopped drinking, partying, and using drugs. I was slowly making up those grades and disciplining myself to make attendance a priority. A college advisor looked at my grades and told me my chances didn't look great but it wasn't impossible. I took my small chance—my tiny shot at college and I went for it. I was one of the first people in my class to get a college acceptance letter. I was blessed enough to receive tuition and board paid for. I finished up the school year and I moved into my college dorm in the Fall. God always has a plan for us even when we are lost in our own self-destruction. Just to put things into perspective no matter what season you're in right now, believe God is at work. Even if you feel like you're at rock bottom God is working.

I'm so grateful God allowed me to go to college but I had to put in the work to meet God halfway. God can't do all the work for us, and it's not because He's not capable but because we have to meet Him halfway for certain assignments in our life. If we are called to start a business or write a book we must pour our labor into what God has asked us to do. Do your part and God will meet you the rest of the way. You can't sit around waiting for God to drop something in your lap because life doesn't work like that. God can redeem us if we've made mistakes and open doors for us but we must take the steps to do our part and put our life back together. The experience of falling behind and making countless mistakes taught me that the Lord could rescue me but He wasn't always going to just hand me success without my willingness and labor.

Even with the publication of this book, I've spent almost two years writing this book. I've watched Heather Lindsey's sermons since my first year of college and now 6 years later her book publishing company is helping me publish this book. God opened the door, but I still had to type the manuscript.

Be not deceived; God is not mocked:
for whatsoever a man soweth, that shall he also reap.
Galatians 6:7

I was a complete mess and not qualified for college by any standards. I was ditching school and I had terrible grades but still, I was capable of redeeming myself and so are you. I didn't have straight A's, but I did have the courage to at least try and believe in myself even if the odds were against me. I was strung out on pills and alcohol several years earlier but still I was sitting in a college classroom. A first-generation college student from the city of Pacoima.

Honestly, I can tell you that God was at work because I had no idea what I was doing in college. I had only planned to graduate from high school but my grandpa always encouraged me to achieve as much as I could despite where I grew up. When you make mistakes in your past or grow up in a certain neighborhood, you'll have labels placed on you and be underestimated. Don't let the enemy keep any negative labels on you. You're allowed to grow and be better. I've learned that people will have opinions about me, but God will have the last word. I care more about what God thinks about me than what people think about me. He can use any story and your story to inspire others so don't give up.

When trying to get back on your feet again understand that when you're rejected from a school or a job that it simply means you're being redirected by God. Learn to have tough skin in this area because to reach success means being rejected and redirected many times. If you're trying to redeem yourself and you feel that you keep failing, just get back up again. God may not open the door you're waiting for because He may want to take time to prepare you for that door. He also might have a better door in mind. Whatever the reason, don't grow frustrated with yourself or God. Learn to develop kindness and patience for yourself.

No matter how many times we fall, God will help us get back again. We are never beyond saving even if we make the same mistakes again and again, God will be there to help us find our way again. Even if a situation is uncomfortable, I believe that God cultivates us during those difficult times, through the heartbreak, betrayal, and through the abandonment. Clearly, God had a much bigger plan than I had for myself. I only imagined myself finishing high school, but God wanted to push me further.

He also intervened at just the right moment and brought me the right people to help me in that particular season in my life. I naturally drifted from other friends that we're going in a different direction. Even our failed relationships can be used to help the women around us. Our wisdom and knowledge can save other women from heartache. Nothing is wasted by God. God is the living water and He can restore any mistake or regret. It's not too late and things are never so bad that you can't redeem yourself, believe me I know. I've fallen in life many times and been able to get back up with God's help. God is wonderful in that way and makes a path for you to start over but you have to take the first step to reach for Him. Even if you've done a considerable amount of damage God can give you life again and He can restore your peace.

Scripture to Meditate

And we know that in all things God works for the good of those who love him, who have been called according to his purpose.

Romans 8:28

For a man who is right with God falls seven times, and rises again, but the sinful fall in time of trouble.

Proverbs 24:16

Prayer

Lord, forgive me for my past choices. Give me wisdom and knowledge moving forward. I know you can take the broken parts of my life and make them beautiful. Restore my heart, mind, and life.

CHAPTER THREE

SPIRITS OF REJECTION AND ABANDONMENT

Whether you have been abandoned by a parent, friend, or lover you know it hurts to be left by someone you care about. Sometimes we internalize and start to list the reasons we think we aren't good enough for someone. We may think we aren't beautiful enough, smart enough, or worthy enough. After it happens once you're afraid it will happen again so you push people away as a way to keep your heart safe or you refuse to put yourself in a position where you will be rejected again. When we're in relationships emotional intimacy becomes a threat and by all costs we avoid it or become overly clingy. Isolation and fear is a tactic used by the enemy to keep us away from love and purpose.

The spirits of rejection keep us from applying to college, dream jobs, promotions, or pursuing healthy relationships. We are paralyzed by the idea that we will be rejected or abandoned by others and when we are in that state of fear whether perceived or real, the dark spirits keep us bound to fear and the enemy wins. But if we decide to take steps toward God, the devil trembles because he knows he will lose his grip on us. The enemy doesn't want to lose us to God. The devil wants us to stay close to Him, paralyzed with fear, anxiety, depression, and low self-esteem but we will no longer fear rejection or abandonment if we are always connected to God. We will see rejection and abandonment through a different lens; we can see it through God's lenses. Rejection will become redirection into God's destiny for us. Abandonment from others will just be God's way of making room for the new people He is going to bring into our lives.

Being abandoned by a parent, friend, or partner hurts. Loving someone and being disappointed by them hurts. Abandonment leaves an emptiness in our soul and we search through life trying to find something or someone to fill the empty space left from a loved one. We roam through life aimlessly trying to figure out why someone didn't love us or fight harder for us and although we can't change our past, we can draw power from our past stories.

We can learn to have authority over the dark spirits trying to invade our mind by first knowing that God will NEVER abandon us or reject us. I'm sure we have all had an experience or memory that made us feel less than adequate but now it's our job to use God's word to reclaim our power over the dark spirits that work tirelessly to keep us in a state of fear.

If we know that God will never leave us then we shouldn't fear if other people reject or abandon us because we know God is with us at all times. God will bring us the people He wants us to be connected to and we won't need to be in a state of fear about losing them. God accepts and loves us. God always works things together for our good, so if we are rejected by a person it's because God has something better in mind. If we're fired from a job or don't get hired for the job of our dreams, it's because God is going to take us to higher places. We never lose when we walk with God. It's hard for our minds to grasp the fact that God always has something better in mind for us. Trust God even when it's hard. I want you to list in your journal all those who have hurt you and give it to God. Start to see the experience through the eyes of God. Sit in prayer and feel God around you. You'll never be alone as long as you have God in your life.

You may not deal with the spirit of rejection or abandonment but you may struggle with fear, depression, or anxiety. Take a mental inventory of the negative spirits trying to have control over your heart and mind. Know that the Lord will go before you and fight your spiritual battles if you ask him to. God is powerful and He can shield you from any darkness. If you're struggling with insecurity, depression, or fear immediately pray and search for scripture in the Bible that focuses on the issues you're struggling with. The Bible and God is your weapon against the enemy. Use the word of God. More importantly remember who you belong to, God. Everything must submit to the name of Jesus, so if you are ever in a very dark moment from your past or present say the name "Jesus" and the enemy will flee.

Scripture to Meditate

Finally, be strong in the Lord and in the strength of his might. Put on the whole armor of God, that you may be able to **stand against the schemes of the devil**. For we do not wrestle against flesh and blood, but against the rulers, against the authorities, against the **cosmic powers over this present darkness, against the spiritual forces of evil** in the heavenly places.
Ephesians 6:10-12

Behold, I have given you authority to tread on serpents and scorpions, and overall the power of the enemy, and nothing shall hurt you.
Luke 10:19

The seventy-two returned with joy, saying, "Lord, even the demons are subject to us in your name!
Luke 10:17

Prayer

I reclaim authority over the spirits of rejection and abandonment. These spirits work to intimidate me and keep me in a constant state of fear. With the name of Jesus, I cast them down. I pray they no longer have power over me. I pray I no longer live in fear of rejection or abandonment. I will not be afraid to be abandoned by anyone because I know God will never abandon me. If someone should reject me, I know God is redirecting for me to something more beautiful.

CHAPTER FOUR

RELATIONSHIP NOT RELIGION

I was never a religious person growing up. As a child, I was never forced to go to church on Sunday and I never went to Sunday school. I only went to church for weddings and funerals. My grandma believed in God but we didn't go to church regularly, she just told me to whisper prayers toward the heavens. I'm certain all her prayers have protected me and I'm grateful for her.

It wasn't until I was at rock bottom that I became desperate for hope and I started praying on my knees. I was going through a difficult time in college and I figured if anyone could help me it was the mysterious God that my grandmother had spoken about in my childhood. During my first year of college, I didn't know anyone at school. God placed me in an uncomfortable situation and I wondered why I was there. I received C's my first semester because I couldn't really find a study system that worked for me. Still, with time I kept studying and trying to do better in my courses. Then I hit a rough patch and returned to my old coping mechanisms because I didn't do the work to heal my childhood and I was pursuing the wrong relationships for affirmation. I made new friends in college and drugs and alcohol became easily accessible again. Social drinking quickly turned into a coping mechanism for feelings of unworthiness and unhealthy relationships.

Things had gotten so bad in my life that I found myself crying out to God while on drugs. I had put myself in a position where I struggled with drugs and alcohol again. I knew I was betraying my soul while pushing my limits with drugs. I was combining different drugs and dating people who were not a good fit for me. I could feel the internal conflict between who I had become and who I knew I had the potential to be. But I was held back by my own destructive habits and the relationships I entertained.

During this time I was also dating a man who was emotionally abusive which didn't help my situation. I was tolerating disrespect daily, frustrated, and crying all the time. I didn't recognize myself and felt out of touch with who I truly was. This guy who we'll call Jake would get upset if I didn't answer his phone calls and he'd guilt trip me for having to study. I had started to become defensive and I would intentionally hurt him verbally and emotionally. I was very toxic in this situation and so was he. He would make me feel bad about not making time for him and try to get my attention by telling me about other women. He also would put my life in danger. One time he picked me up while he was drunk and I didn't notice until he started swerving out of the driving lane. I realized he had beer cans in the backseat but still I didn't want to leave him because I didn't want him to get into an accident. He was yelling and so was I. As his emotions began to pour out, he uttered: "One day I'm not going to be here for you to come back to because you treat me bad." It was at that moment that I realized how broken we both were.

Out of desperation, I started going to a church near my college dorm. I would stop by during weekdays only for a few minutes in hopes that a loud voice would erupt from the ceiling with all my answers. To my disappointment, a voice never erupted, and I would return to my car feeling I couldn't find this mysterious God. I never went to a church service because I thought the building itself was a cure enough. I went to many different churches searching for God until one day my mother invited me to her church.

I was still hurt with her from my childhood and I was still carrying a lot of resentment. We had never really discussed the pain she had caused me so I didn't want to seek God with her. God works in miraculous ways because He used my mother to draw me into a relationship with Him so don't be surprised how God draws you to Him. It doesn't always happen the way you think it will.

My mother would invite me to church and every Sunday I refused to go with her. She had been going to this church for a while and her heart was changing even if I was too prideful to admit it at the time. She was praying over me constantly and I shrugged off her prayers and her new relationship with the Lord. I had always seen her as the villain. I wanted to keep being angry with her for the abandonment in my childhood although she apologized fervently for leaving.

Still, I would kindly deny every weekend because I wasn't ready to forgive her yet. Before I would even consider the invitation, I'd think of work and school assignments and that alone was enough for me to say no. At the time I thought of church as an inconvenience to my Sunday morning. I had been partying all weekend and Sunday was my day to rest.

Finally, after months of my mother praying over me, I finally went to church with her. Things had become so dark in my life that I didn't have a choice but to reach for my mom's God. I was taking different types of drugs in a single night and fearing that I would die in my sleep. I had to ask my roommates to check if I was breathing when they woke up because I'd most likely be asleep until noon. They wouldn't have known if I overdosed in the middle of the night because it was common for me to sleep until noon.

The first time I walked into my mom's church, I cried. Nina, a beautiful singer that leads worship at my church started to sing and I cried. My mother had been raving about Nina for months but I couldn't understand what she was talking about until I heard Nina sing for myself. I hadn't felt comfort and peace in a very long time but when I heard her voice, I felt just that.

The worship team elicited such a beautiful feeling in me that I could never again doubt that there was a God and He knew exactly where I needed to be. It was the feeling that I had been searching for in bars, parties, and men. It was God's comfort and the strong love that I felt in church among His people. The Holy Spirit touched my heart and I cried unashamedly in a room filled with people for the first time. It was indescribable and I thought everyone would look over at me and stare. However, everyone was looking toward the worship team or raising their hands toward Heaven. Everyone was sharing their own personal moments with God. I looked over at my mother who had her hands raised and watched as she cried. I suspect that she was thanking God that I had finally come back into the light.

As I looked toward the worship team again, I heard Nina sing "The Lord leaves the ninety-nine to find you". I knew the Lord was talking to me directly. That song refers to a parable in the Bible. In the parable, Jesus explains if a shepherd loses one sheep won't he leave the other ninety-nine sheep in his flock to go find the one that is lost and wandering. We are God's sheep and when we are lost, He will come to find us.

If a man has a hundred sheep and one of them wanders away, what will he do? Won't he leave the ninety-nine others on the hills and go out to search for the one that is lost?

Matthew 18:12

This church was different than anything I had ever experienced before. People hugged at the beginning of service and I was put off because I wasn't much of a hugger. I think people could sense that, so they shook my hand to still make me feel welcomed. While I was attending church more frequently—along with reading the Bible— I could slowly start to feel light come into the cracks of my life and slowly I stopped the drugs, drinking, and partying. I could feel myself developing into a different woman and with that change came the loss of the things God no longer wanted in my life.

I haven't left that church since. My mother prayed for my healing while I was in the darkness. I'm so thankful for her because my relationship has been able to flourish with her and with God. As I kept getting closer to God, I could feel things with my romantic relationship and friendships getting worse. I was hoping things would improve but they didn't. I was outgrowing most of the people in my life and it was because God was taking me to a new level. I couldn't understand at the time, but it was God trying to pull me away from that relationship and friendships that were hindering my overall growth. That's the thing about friendships and relationships that God didn't create for long term purposes, they will not prosper, and I learned that the hard way.

As I started to get closer to God, I thought prayer would mend my relationship. Jake thought it was silly to pray for him because he didn't believe in God but still I prayed over us. Prayer was a gesture of mine that he dismissed. He felt God hadn't done anything for him and asking God for help was silly. I think it became clear to both of us that we weren't going to prosper in a relationship. After months of trying to understand each other and it not working out, we threw in the towel. After some time when the heartache subsided the Holy Spirit told me "He wasn't the man that you could build your life with". When I started going to church, I was praying for that relationship to work out but what God was really doing was drawing me closer to Him. He was creating a woman who would chase after His own heart and fiercely love Him.

I was starting to make new friends at church which took some time because I was an introvert. For months I just ran out of service without getting to know anyone. Then one day Nina, the worship singer started to reach out to me. We started to talk more and slowly I began to develop new friendships in the church. I could instantly tell the difference between my bar friends and my church friends.

At the time I still had one foot in, one foot out when it came to church. I didn't change overnight, and it may be the same for you. I was still going to bars during my first steps in this journey and hanging out with my old friends. I thought if I really stepped in with God it meant that I couldn't have fun anymore but being lost in a drunken state surrounded by other lost people in a dark mental place isn't fun. I want to be transparent with you because I want you to know you can come to Jesus just as you are. You don't need to be perfect to come to Jesus, that's not how it works. No matter what your life looks like right now or what you're struggling with you can come to Jesus, there is no need to wait until you think you're perfect.

It's important to build a relationship with God and not religion. An example of someone who only seeks religion would be someone who shows up to church thinking they will earn "Heaven points" for only showing up but continue to be mean to people throughout the week and dishonor God. I've met people in church who serve yet are really unkind and judgmental when you get to know them. I've also known people who may not go to church every Sunday but have an active prayer life and reflect God in every area of their life. They are in a relationship with Jesus and actively seeking Him by reading His word and demonstrating the fruits of the spirit like kindness, love, and selflessness.

Building a relationship with Jesus is like building a friendship. He is Father, friend, comforter, and creator of all. You can tell Him everything and anything. You can pray for things and cry to Him and you have access to Him at all times. He can help you heal your past and break generational curses off your life. Anything negative you've heard about God from others, disregard it. Seek Him for yourself and get to know him on a personal level. Read the Bible and spend time with Him. A relationship requires that you pour energy and time into getting to know someone. Learn to trust Him and rely on Him.

I want you to know life with Jesus is a journey and it will take time for the Lord to heal all areas of your life and change your habits. God is not asking you to be perfect overnight but He will challenge you to be a better version of yourself and let go of your past unhealthy habits. He asks us not to sin because it is not in our best interest to sin. We are the ones that struggle with guilt, fear, anxiety, and depression after sin.

That is why the Bible says stay clear of sin. We are human and we will make mistakes but it is in our best interest to challenge ourselves to let go of what God is asking us to let go of and refrain from making the same mistakes. Our relationship with God and following His word in the Bible is for our own joy and peace. God wants us to have peace and He gave us the Bible to help us have the key to life.

When I started to feel that I needed to be perfect for God it discouraged me from a relationship with Him altogether. God asks us to just take one step at a time so be patient with yourself. Little by little the Holy Spirit started to transform me and I started to go out less. The last few times I got really drunk I felt the Holy Spirit tell me: "You've outgrown this place and I've designed you for more." Then naturally I lost all those old friendships that came with drinking.

No church is perfect but I can say our environment is important. It's important to know that people go to church to heal so it's not a perfect place. Some people are dealing with insecurity, jealousy, rage, pain, negative thoughts, or resentment. People are praying for health problems, loved ones, or financial issues. Not everyone will be pleasant because they are going to church to heal so it's important to keep that in mind. Some people in the church will let you down but remember that you are going there for God. However, our immediate circle of friends is our own personal garden. Who we choose to spend our time with and where we choose to spend our time creates our life. Surround yourself with people who add value to your life and uplift you. Rejoice with God's people and get to know Jesus for yourself.

Being in church and being in the presence of the Lord on Sunday is a way that you can replenish and renew yourself for the rest of the week. You're not earning points with God if you go to church on Sunday but in your heart, you don't want to be there. God knows our hearts. Seeking God with prayer and reading scripture is really for your own well-being. You are the person that will benefit from getting closer to God. He will give you the tools to balance life, joy, and peace in your life.

Scripture to Meditate

but whoever drinks of the water that I will give him shall never thirst; but the water that I will give him will become in him a well of water springing up to eternal life."
John 4:14

My son, do not forget my teaching, but keep my commands in your heart, for they will prolong your life many years and bring you peace and prosperity. Let love and faithfulness never leave you; bind them around your neck, write them on the tablet of your heart. Then you will win favor and a good name in the sight of God and man.
Proverbs 3:1-4

You will seek me and find me, when you seek me with all your heart.
Jeremiah 29:13

But they who wait for the Lord shall renew their strength; They shall mount up with wings like eagles; They shall run and not be weary; They shall walk and not faint.
Isaiah 40:31

And whoever does not take his cross and follow me is not worthy of me. Whoever finds his life will lose it, and whoever loses his life for my sake will find it.
Matthew 10:38-39

The fear of the Lord leads to life, and whoever has it rests satisfied; he will not be visited by harm.

Proverbs 19:23

"The kingdom of Heaven is like treasure hidden in a field, which a man found and covered up. Then in his joy he goes and sells all that he has and buys that field. "Again, the kingdom of Heaven is like a merchant in search of fine pearls, who, on finding one pearl of great value, went and sold all that he had and bought it."

Matthew 13: 44-46

Prayer

Lord, help me to break any barriers that have kept me away from you. Help me to unlearn any biases or versions of you that I've learned from other people. I've heard about you but I want to know you personally Lord. Give me the opportunity to know you from my own experience and teach me to build a relationship with you.

CHAPTER FIVE

LORD, CHANGE MY HEART

When I first started my journey toward healing, God revealed aspects of my personality that needed to be changed. I was angry, sad, jealous, and insecure most of early adulthood. My behavior toward others was very cruel especially toward the people I loved most. I was unforgiving, sarcastic, and angry all the time. I could be careless with my words and if I felt disrespected in any way I would say the first hurtful thing that could hurt the person I was arguing with. I was using words to tear others down because of my own insecurities. I operated mostly from a place of ego and I was very unkind.

When I spoke to people, I didn't reflect Jesus at all. I've hurt many people emotionally along the way but luckily with the conviction of the Holy Spirit, I've been able to change. After I started reading the Bible more, I had to discipline myself to hold back certain responses that I was accustomed to. I noticed that the more I stepped toward God the more love began to flow out of me toward others and the more I felt convicted by the Holy Spirit to be kind and generous toward others. I became much more confident, graceful, and gentle.

I have learned from my personal experience that those who are unkind have anger stored up in their hearts and their hate flows out toward others. The same is true for us, when we are filled with anger, hurt, bitterness, and jealousy it flows out onto others.

A good man brings good things out of the good stored up in his heart, and an evil man brings evil things out of the evil stored up in his heart. For the mouth speaks what the heart is full of.
Luke 6:45

Once I started to walk with God I could feel the Holy Spirit tug on my heart whenever I was cruel to someone or insensitive and immediately ask for forgiveness. When you start a relationship with God you'll know when you're doing something out of alignment with God because the Holy Spirit will pull on you to do the right thing. The Holy Spirit will tug on you and challenge you to overcome your old ways. If we want to become who God wants us to be it will require us to give up old unhealthy ways of thinking and behaviors.

God started to unteach me old behaviors and attitudes that I had learned from my friends, environment, and family. Just because we aren't hurting someone physically doesn't mean we're not hurting someone emotionally. We have no idea how long someone carries hurtful words with them or the potential that words have to lead someone else into depression.

With the help of the Holy Spirit and Jesus I now have the ability to change unhealthy habits, behaviors, and my old way of thinking and so will you. If we want to know how God wants us to act toward others we can find it in the Bible. The Bible has taught me the qualities I want to possess as a God-loving woman. I want to have fruits of the spirit that demonstrate kindness, patience, and love. Our personalities and behaviors are a direct reflection of how deeply rooted in God we are. If we are truly rooted in God then love should flow from us.

The Bible uses a specific parable to demonstrate the fruits of our spirit. The parable compares humans to trees and it explains that a good tree bears good fruit but a bad tree bears bad fruit. If we are trees rooted in God we should bear kindness, love, empathy, hope, faith, and forgiveness. If we are rooted in the world, we will bear hate, anger, and judgment. We should strive to be the best versions of ourselves and that means outgrowing the past versions of ourselves that no longer serve us. When you come to the Lord you can guarantee that He will send you tests to help you achieve the fruits of the spirit. He may send you a situation that requires you to be patient when you struggle with being patient.

Once you're aware that your actions hurt God and others, it's your responsibility to pray and make an adjustment. I personally struggled with a volatile mood and I had to ask God to help me manage my temperament. Growing up I was surrounded by volatile personalities and I had the same issue. The good thing about awareness is that you can change it with God's help. Once I had the Holy Spirit if I was unkind the amount of guilt I felt afterward was unbearable because I'd go over the situation in my mind over and over again, knowing that it was probably something that I shouldn't have said in the first place. God has the power to renew our minds and change our old ways of speaking. Before God, we are a prisoner to our old ways of thinking but after God, we become more of a reflection of Him.

I also struggled with forgiveness. I was always free to say whatever I want and expect forgiveness from others but when someone else said something to hurt my feelings I couldn't forgive. My wonderful friends loved and accepted me during this time but I always saw forgiveness as a form of weakness. If someone hurt me and I forgave them, I felt a sense of weakness. I could really hold a grudge even for the smallest betrayal. If I did somehow allow you to stay in my life after a betrayal, I would always bring up the incident. I'd make sure the person would suffer by making the other person feel guilty. I would bring up the betrayal in conversation again and again. Never letting it go. I could also cut someone out of my life and not even give it a second thought, consciously knowing firsthand the damage that abandonment could inflict on someone. It was spiritually draining to live with this much anger, hurt, and unforgiveness in my heart.

Being angry is a normal emotion but hurting people while angry is not something God wants us to do. Hurting others is how we send hatred back into the world and plant negative seeds into the lives of others. Hate and anger is the way the enemy uses each of us as his own personal vessel to harm others. We raise our voice, speak without knowing the damage we may potentially inflict in the lives of others. There was so much work that had to be done in my heart but God worked on different issues at different times. Slowly, He started to change my heart and the way I behaved toward others. The Holy Spirit was also influential in changing my heart. Whenever I said something mean or did something that didn't reflect Jesus, I felt internal conflict. I didn't feel better until I asked for forgiveness from God or from the person I hurt.

The Bible has taught me to love others fiercely and pray over them. I want them to know Jesus and be healed so they can bear good fruit in the world and have long-lasting peace in their lives. Each of us can do that by bearing good fruit in our life and demonstrating love to others. I've walked with the Lord for some time and the Holy Spirit still reminds me when I'm behaving in a way that doesn't honor God.

When I first started my walk with God I thought I would never hurt anyone again but I had to learn to give myself the space to understand that I would still make mistakes although I had given my heart to God. He wasn't going to change me overnight because it's a process. At the beginning of my journey, I was constantly in fear that I was disappointing God all the time but that was a lie. We are human so we will make mistakes, the only perfect person is Jesus Christ. God knows you better than you know yourself. He knew exactly who you were when you came to Him. That is why He called you to Him in the first place because He wants to help any negative parts of yourself that are hurting you and others. I want to encourage you to be patient and kind to yourself during your walk. You will make mistakes but God still loves you regardless. Do not be discouraged at all because God is forgiving and loving despite what you've learned about him. The battle against the spirit trying to enslave you to your past belongs to the Lord. Your part is to pray and watch as God helps you win your mental battles against those spirits. You will be incredibly proud of the woman God will transform you into.

Scripture to Meditate

Do not be afraid or discouraged, for the battle is not yours, but God's.
2 Chronicles 20:15

Do not conform to the pattern of this world, but be transformed by the renewing of your mind. Then you will be able to test and approve what God's will is—his good, pleasing and perfect will.
Romans 12:2

For at one time you were darkness, but now you are light in the Lord. Walk as children of light
Ephesians 5:8

Prayer

Lord, I pray you renew my mind. Help me to reflect more of you Jesus. Please change anything about myself that doesn't reflect you. I pray that I change my behaviors, habits, and mindset. Lord help me to let go of any aspects of myself that no longer serve me. In Jesus' name, Amen.

CHAPTER SIX

DATING

Who we choose to date is important and who we choose to marry is important. We should be careful about the men we allow into our lives. If we aren't conscious about who we spend our time with we can be potentially giving the devil an open door into our life through another person. We create our own personal Heaven or hell by who we choose to start relationships with and if we date carelessly we may subject ourselves to unnecessary heartache and separation from God.

Sometimes we're led into relationships because of a "spark". We get lonely or feel affirmed because someone is giving us attention. We see someone who catches our eye or a man who gives us some validation by pursuing us and we call that a spark. We make decisions to jump into relationships too quickly because of that spark but the spark alone isn't enough to build a relationship foundation with. We look for that spark when we first meet someone but what people don't tell you is that the spark doesn't mean someone is qualified by God to be in a relationship with you. The spark can just be a moment of lust or attraction but it eventually subsides. It is our job to look past the momentary spark. We must evaluate the character, actions, and values of a man. That is the true way to see if he is a good fit for you and see whether that is someone you can build a life with. More importantly, you can find out if that person is someone God wants you to build a life with. I believe if you seek God about your romantic life He'll give you discernment about whether the man you're interested in is the man He wants you to be in relationship with.

At the beginning of a relationship, there can also be red flags that we overlook because we're so attracted to the external appearance of a person. When you learn that you're loved by God you don't jump at the first man that gives you attention. When you know and experience God's love you know exactly how you should be treated by a man. God treats us with kindness, compassion, empathy, forgiveness, and care. He is someone we can trust and depend on during hard times and those are similar qualities that we should be looking for in men.

If the man you're dating is rude, unkind, quick to anger, inconsiderate, stop right there. Habits and patterns shown in the beginning are a tell-tell how he is going to treat you the rest of the relationship. If he's known for cheating, womanizing, and has a wandering eye, stop right there. I believe people can change but I wouldn't risk your heart on "what if he changes". What if he doesn't? Are you prepared for the heartache for the rest of your life? If he's leaving you on read and is inconsistent with his communication with you that's not someone who is clear about his intentions with you. I understand that people get busy but if there's no explanation and if it happens more than twice, life is too short to be asking for someone's love crumbs. The man God wants you to spend your life with will not give you his crumbs he will make it very transparent that you are a priority in his life.

Most of the women in my life and myself have countless stories of staying in unhealthy relationships and tolerating nonsense for way too long. We lower our standards, become complacent with disrespect, or give too much of ourselves to men who weren't qualified to be in a relationship with us from the beginning. I don't mean to sound pretentious but there are absolutely some people who we shouldn't be in relationships with romantically because they aren't a match for us. A way to avoid being hurt is to love yourself, your time, and how hard you've worked to be the woman you are. If you love yourself, you don't just give yourself to the lowest bidder; by lowest bidder I mean the man who is only going to invest the least amount emotionally, spiritually, and mentally.

Each of us has a story. Maybe picking the wrong partner out of loneliness or desperation. Maybe we got into a relationship with a man who was great in the beginning and suddenly he is someone you don't recognize anymore. When that relationship ends we're left to deal with a heartbreak that sometimes lasts for months or years. Instead of using that time as an opportunity for healing, people avoid loneliness and jump into a new unhealthy relationship with whoever is available next. I personally never ran out of suitors and I kept dating. My emotional baggage kept accumulating and my emotions were scattered everywhere because I never gave myself a chance to heal. I would ignore all those first red flags about the new man because I was desperately trying to repress the disappointment of the last man.

I strongly recommend healing your heart before jumping into a new relationship. Learn to stand firm with God. Once I started pursuing God I stopped seeking unhealthy partners. God had the space to heal my heart and I stopped carrying emotional baggage and childhood bondage into new relationships. Before God, I never had a chance to heal my heart and a relationship would turn out one of two ways.

I would start dating a nice guy and hold him accountable for all the mistakes of the last guy I dated. If I was cheated on by the last man, I wasn't able to trust the new person because I hadn't healed before jumping into a new relationship. I would act out of jealousy and insecurity. I would start arguments that stemmed from my own insecurity. Even if the other person didn't give me any reason not to trust him, I just couldn't trust. I was only able to love others through the broken parts of myself. Even if the relationship was going well, I would decide to end things because the spirit of abandonment could only get me to a certain point in a relationship, I call it the point of no return. The point of no return is the point in the relationship where you're all in so if things end it's going to be messy and painful. So I would abort the mission before I got to the point of no return.

In the second scenario, I would get into a relationship with a bad guy out of desperation and that was the roller coaster of hell. When you're desperate for a relationship you ignore all the red flags and you jump in and out of relationships to feel a sense of worthiness. I found myself tolerating unfaithfulness, irresponsibility, and lack of consideration with some not so great guys. Being in an unhealthy relationship made my life so much harder.

I somehow felt my worth was connected to dating someone. I couldn't build intimacy with anyone nor did I want to. I dated nice guys who wanted to help me emotionally, but I wasn't in a position to enter a healthy relationship. My perception of a normal relationship was seriously flawed. I thought if I felt afraid and anxious from my partners' avoidant tendencies that it meant I was in the right relationship. I dated not so great guys and I wanted to make things work with them but it never worked. Bringing two broken people together is usually a disaster.

Women are resilient, beautiful, and intellectual yet we get into relationships with men who aren't sent from God. Some men haven't done the work to heal themselves emotionally or mentally so they aren't qualified to meet us where we are in life. Some men have zero ambition and don't take steps to pursue their goals. Other men don't treat us well but we stay in the relationship feeling it's our obligation to help them grow while they're damaging us emotionally. We fall in love with a man's potential or the idea of happily ever after. We take on the role of mother and wife right from the beginning without evaluating if the man in front of us is our equal or approved by God.

You are under no obligation to raise a grown man. If he is more of a burden than a light in your life while dating, let him go. He will hinder you, your growth, and your career. If you meet a man that isn't perfect but you know in your heart that he is in alignment with God's will for your life, pray to God about it. It's important to evaluate a man's character, values, and ambitions. Don't invent a pretend man in your head to match your fantasy of the perfect guy. Listen to his words and evaluate his actions. Does he keep his promises? Is he just trying to have sex? Is he honoring your boundaries? Does he make you a priority? Is he ambitious? Does he know how to love? Is he making an effort to heal any past traumas?

If you are in an unhealthy relationship and things aren't getting better, seek God. If someone is repeatedly hurting you emotionally, it's not healthy to stay in the relationship. Take an inventory of how you feel now, how you've felt lately. Not how you felt when the relationship started. Don't continue to lie to yourself because it is only you who will hurt.

Dating with Intention

I think women and men should date with intention. If you've been hurt like me, you get to a point where you're over it. You're over the tears, heartbreak, and frustration. If you're going to date someone make sure that it's with the intention of long-term. Make sure he is someone who you like from the beginning. I don't know about you but I don't want to spend four years with a man only to find out he had no intention of marrying me to begin with. I'm also not a Band-Aid for broken men to use me to fill a void in their life. Remember every time you casually date you're putting your heart at risk and the Bible says, "Guard your heart" so I would advise you to have intention when you're dating people. Never be afraid to ask a man where you're heading in a relationship. If he doesn't see a relationship with you long-term it means that he's just using you as a way to fill a void or just to pass the time with. You don't want to pour all your energy and love into a man that doesn't feel the same about you.

Seek God about your romantic relationships. This is one of the most important decisions of your life. It is better to be single with God than in a relationship that is out of God's will for your life. Who you marry will affect you and your children. Do not take this decision lightly and do not just seek a relationship to fill the loneliness.

Scripture to Meditate

Do not be unequally yoked with unbelievers. For what partnership has righteousness with lawlessness? Or what fellowship has light with darkness?

2 Corinthians 6:14

As iron sharpens iron, so one person sharpens another.

Proverbs 27:17

Dating Prayer

Single

Lord, help me to only be in relationships that are covered and ordained by you. Please allow only the relationships sent by you to flourish and give me the wisdom to trust you in my romantic life. I pray I wait on you Lord rather than make decisions without you that may lead me into heartbreak. Protect me from the relationships that lead me away from you. Help me be patient in this single season. In Jesus' name, Amen.

In a Relationship

Lord, I pray that my relationship is covered by you. I pray that we both are seeking your will for our lives. I pray that we seek you every step of our relationship. I pray you cover my partner and protect him from the things trying to harm him or any darkness trying to hinder our connection to you. In Jesus' name, Amen.

CHAPTER SEVEN

DIMMING YOUR LIGHT FOR MEN

I've always heard relationships are give and take but I always found myself compromising so much of myself in relationships. I was always the one sacrificing or conforming to make the other person happy. I had a habit of dismissing my needs, values, and concerns to avoid any friction in the relationship. There were moments I would put my personal growth on hold to build the other person into a better man. I had a habit of believing in a man without any real evidence that he wanted to grow or change into a better version of himself. God always asks us to be the best version of ourselves and He uplifts us. If God is always encouraging us to go higher, why do we spend time with people who want us to be smaller to make them comfortable?

I've shrunk myself in a few relationships because I didn't want to be "too smart" or "too ambitious". I didn't want to take away from a man's masculinity so I dimmed my light. There was this one incident that taught me to never dim my light to make someone else feel comfortable because it was an act of self-betrayal. I was in college and Jake wasn't. He worked a labor job which I had no issue with because all the men in my family worked labor jobs. He hadn't gone to college but he was still one of the smartest men I had ever met up to that point. He was self-aware, opinionated, and passionate about his work. He was introspective and he helped me to become more self-aware but for some reason, it bothered him that I was pursuing a college degree. He would make snarky remarks about how he wasn't given the same opportunities or say that I thought I was better than him, which wasn't true at all. I admired his intelligence even without a college degree.

This guy also loved to go out and drink all the time. I spent the majority of the time studying but once in a while I would go out and drink with him. I couldn't honor myself and see clearly that this person wasn't a good fit for me. I didn't enjoy drinking or being out till 4 a.m. every weekend because I'm a homebody. I had spent the first two years of college making mistakes, so I wanted to finish my last years of college strong academically. I was in college and chasing after my dreams, but this person was comfortable with being complacent and it held me back. I was always frustrated so we would fight all the time and rather than end things which should have been the obvious choice to make because eventually, we would just grow apart anyway, I stayed in the relationship.

I believe a significant other either builds you up or holds you back. Learn and study yourself very well and know who will align with your personality and know who you are before getting into a relationship. If you're ambitious don't get into a relationship with someone who isn't because it will frustrate you or you'll find yourself dimming yourself down so that the relationship will run smoothly.

Little by little my inner light started to dim. I would feel guilty and downplay my accomplishments to make him feel comfortable in the relationship. I was playing small and dumbing myself down all the time and he would still manage to find something that made him feel emasculated. During a heated argument, he said: "I want to feel like a man when I walk into a room with you and I can't feel that." That was the moment I realized he was dealing with his own insecurity and that had nothing to do with me. I replied: "It's not my fault you're insecure about who you are."

That was the last time I ever dimmed myself for anyone else. God asks us to be the greatest versions of ourselves. He asks us to be bold and fearless women chasing after Him and our purpose. Don't let relationships that aren't qualified by God to influence the woman you can be. Be confident in who you are and own it, don't let these men steal your light. If a man intentionally makes you feel dumb or tells you that you aren't beautiful—drop him! Any man that can say or do those kinds of things isn't sent by God to be in a healthy relationship with you. Don't allow any man to make you feel less than you are. If God wouldn't speak to you that way, don't let your partner.

There was another time I dated a wealthy guy who came from a wealthy family. I was a bit younger than him and felt that I had to be a different woman around him. I'd be self-possessed and placed ridiculously high expectations on myself to act the part in his life. I was in a state of needing to impress others. I grew up in the San Fernando Valley in the city of Pacoima. I can be eloquent in speech, but I'm also opinionated. If you're rude to others I have no problem correcting, you and I speak my truth. I speak up for others if I feel someone else is hurting them verbally or being a bully. I'm a God-loving, college-educated woman but I'm not ashamed to say I grew up in the valley. Any of the men I've dated can attest to it, I have always spoken my mind and my truth. But around him, I felt that I needed to be refined and eloquent to maintain the relationship with him and that didn't work out either because I was pretending to be someone I wasn't.

Date men who lift you higher, not men who need to put you down to feel like men. Also, don't feel you need to be a completely different person to make someone else happy. Date someone that is much more aligned with you opposed to trying to force yourself to be someone God didn't ask you to be.

If you're ambitious pay attention to a man's work ethic and his actions. Don't date the guy that always talks about starting a business but takes no steps toward getting a business license or saving for a company. There are plenty of "talkers" but rarely are there people who follow through with what they say when it comes to goals. Ask a man while you're getting to know him, "What actions are you taking to pursue your goals?" If he's always on social media, always drinking, hanging out with friends, and chasing after girls, trust me, he will waste your time.

Build a life with someone who can keep up with your dreams and ambitions. Pay attention to a man that respects your time and values. Spend life with a man that can hold his own spiritually, financially, and mentally. Don't build a life with someone who you have to dim your light for and don't feel you need to apologize for your ambition, beauty, or intelligence.

I now refuse to make myself small to make anyone else happy. Whether that is a friend, family member, or romantic partner. Take a moment to think about those in your life that are dimming your light. I want you to know that those kinds of relationships and friendships will fall apart because you aren't being true to yourself. Spend time with people who help you flourish and grow.

Shrinking myself to make others comfortable was also holding back the woman that God created me to be. God created me with ambition and a thirst for knowledge. God has a person for you that is your equal. The wrong man can fill us with insecurity and doubt about ourselves. The devil can distract us from our purpose by placing the wrong man in front of us, breaking down the woman God created us to be—speaking death into us instead of life. I don't believe it's a radical idea to say that God has someone that will be your equal and someone who will compliment you and your personality. But I do believe that if we're in a relationship with someone God didn't design for us we won't be able to receive our equal and we'll continue to lie to ourselves that the person in front of us is who God wants us to be with but feel all the hurt and disappointment of being in the wrong relationship.

Always be true to yourself. I have accepted that I'm not perfect and I've learned to challenge myself to overcome weaknesses. But don't feel you need to conform to the standards of others to fit in their life. God doesn't ask us to bow down to other people and be who others think we should be. God asks us to submit to Him and be who He says we should be. Remember other people can lead you into destruction. If you are outgrowing a relationship you can't force someone to grow with you nor should you ever play small to make someone else happy. You won't have to conform or play small for the person God wants you to be with.

Ride or Die Woman

The ride or die narrative is the idea that women should tolerate abuse, manipulation, and mistreatment to achieve the "ride or die" title from men. It has been constructed by men to benefit men and I want to dismantle this idea that women should sacrifice their emotional well-being and soul for men. We should only be giving that much of ourselves to God.

When I was dating Jake, he would measure my love for him based on how much abuse I could tolerate. I would avoid arguing with him and he would say, "You don't care enough." One time I was studying for a college final and he was yelling at me over the phone because I didn't coddle him for his bad decisions. Every weekend it was something new. He was either in a bar fight, thrown in jail, or I wasn't giving him enough attention. After a long conversation, he said: "You aren't ride or die." I was insulted and I felt my femininity being attacked. I started to second guess my ability to support him through thick and thin. My culture and neighborhood had placed so much value in being able to support a man no matter the circumstances. That meant staying in an unhealthy relationship even if it was costing your peace and emotional health. I want to be the one to tell you that God will not ask you to stay in relationships that are hurting you emotionally all the time if you're dating. He will not ask you to tolerate a man cheating on you all the time. He doesn't want to keep you in relationships that keep you away from peace and joy.

Society has taught men that a woman who tolerates anything is a woman who truly loves him instead of teaching him not to put a woman through so much heartache to begin with. I dated Jake casually for two years, bear with me I wasn't making the best judgments and we've all been there. He would project his anger onto me. He wanted me to feel sorry for him and I couldn't. Men either make moves or make excuses. It was very clear how he wanted to spend his time but I didn't have time to waste. I don't have the time nor the energy to coddle a grown man who isn't willing to pick himself up. Luckily God tore that relationship apart and we both moved on with our lives.

I want to tell you that you don't need to compromise your relationship with God or the relationship you have with yourself for an unhealthy relationship. Don't think you need to put your feelings on the back burner to keep still waters in a relationship. If a man doesn't think you're a ride or die because you don't tolerate his nonsense, that's fine. Let him find someone else that will and pray for her. I'd much rather be a woman of God than a ride or die woman. God doesn't want you to stretch yourself and break your soul to win the approval of a man. If you feel that you're sacrificing your heart then pray and ask God to release you from that unhealthy relationship. We don't need to be ride or die women, we need to be women who are willing to obey God when He is asking us to let go of a relationship.

Scripture to Meditate

Do not be conformed to this world, but be transformed by the renewal of your mind, that by testing you may discern what is the will of God, what is good and acceptable and perfect.

Romans 12:2

He who walks with wise men will be wise, But the companion of fools will suffer harm.

Proverbs 13:20

Leave the presence of a fool, for there you do not meet words of knowledge.

Proverbs 14:7

Prayer

Heavenly Father, I pray I don't dim my inner light for others. I pray I'm confident in you who you created me to be. I pray I'm not swayed or discouraged by the negative opinions of others. Lord, help me prosper and build relationships that help me step into the woman you want me to be. Bring people in my life that encourage me and uplift me. In Jesus' name, amen.

CHAPTER EIGHT

MEN WILL NOT HEAL US

Women in my life and society have always portrayed men as the answer to all of our problems but that has never been the case. When I saw people getting into new relationships I thought they found the answer to healing so I assumed a man would be the key to my healing, only to find myself in an unhealthy relationship months later leading into more brokenness. I used men, alcohol, drugs, status, but nothing worked to heal my heart. I would feel a momentary high or a brief moment of significance but the feeling of unworthiness still lingered in the back of my mind. We're sold this idea that men alone will make us happy and that has led many of us into heartbreak. I believe love is beautiful, I'm certainly not a pessimist. But I know from experience that the hands of man are too fragile and too small to heal us in ways only God can. I want to lead you to a love that will never fail you, the love of God. You will never again fear losing a relationship and you'll learn not to put all your worth in a man.

First, I want to say you're whole and affirmed in Jesus Christ. Repeat it and believe it. You don't need a man to feel worthybecause the Creator of the universe thinks you're worthy. You're here on earth which means that God made you with a specific purpose and it is certainly not to go around asking men to affirm you. I used to think a man praising me in a relationship would make me feel worthy and whole. I thought I was only valuable if someone else said so. There have been many times I've rushed ahead of God to fill my emptiness and start dating the wrong person only to feel more empty in the relationship. Most people only feel valuable, affirmed, and important when they're in a relationship and that is why some of us are just participating in superficial relationships. These relationships don't last long and lack depth. When those relationships reach their limitation and it's over, we're left with emptiness. I used to put all my hope in men thinking that they would somehow fill what I was missing but that was an area that only God could fill. Thinking men had the answer has led me to a long path of disappointment. Some men are conditioned by cultural norms to be hyper-masculine and disconnected from their emotions. Men can be emotionally unavailable, disrespectful, or irresponsible. Okay, so not all men are like this but I had a pattern when I dated so I'm talking about the sample size from my dating life. I was hoping for one of them to save me? They were just as lost as I was. Sometimes even a little more lost than I was.

I spent a decade thinking men somehow had the answer to what I had been searching for. We've all grown up with this fantasy that once this special person comes into our life that all is well in the world and we reach wholeness. I started to think every man was "the man" that would lead to my wholeness, only to be disappointed again a few months later. Real wholeness comes from knowing we are loved so much by God.

The best thing about leaning on God to fill the void in my life was that God would never break up with me or abandon me. Even if I was having a hard day, I knew that God loved me that day just as much as He did the day before. I learned I had 24-hour access to God through prayer and reading the Bible. I talked to Him whenever I felt anxious or whenever I remembered painful memories. He can do the same for you. Jesus has the power to calm the storms in your mind and give your heart peace when you feel anxious.

I started rechanneling the energy that I usually poured into men and I put the energy into finishing college, writing this book, and emotionally healing. The same spot that once held a void became the same spot where God began to work and manifest beauty. I know that He will do the same for you if you give Him the chance. Placing our healing in the hands of others will not work, we must seek God to heal and restore our heart if we want long-lasting healing. Unhealthy coping mechanisms can only work for a moment, but Jesus can help our healing last long-term. It's our responsibility to invite God to heal us. The longer we try to use others to heal us the longer we will be disappointed. Look to God, not to people.

Scripture to Meditate

Be not dismayed, for I am with you. I will not fail you or forsake you, wherever you go. Be strong and of good courage.
Deuteronomy 31:6

I sought the Lord and He heard me and delivered me from all of my fears.
Psalm 34:4

Then suddenly a woman . . . came up behind him and touched the fringe of his cloak, for she said to herself, 'If I only touch his cloak, I will be made well.' Jesus turned, and seeing her he said, 'Take heart, daughter; your faith has made you well.
Matthew 9:20–22

When Jesus entered Peter's house, he saw his mother-in-law lying in bed with a fever; he touched her hand, and the fever left her, and she got up and began to serve him.
Matthew 8:14–15

Prayer

Lord, help me to put my worth and value in you alone. I pray I don't put others before you. Help me to remember that only you can heal me. Help me to put my faith in you God. In Jesus' name, Amen.

CHAPTER NINE

SETTLING IN RELATIONSHIPS

The main reason I believe people settle in relationships is because they don't know how much they're loved by God. I know for a fact that God has more for us than we could ever imagine, it is us that feel we don't deserve happiness. Some of us have been in a series of bad relationships and think it's normal to be unhappy in a relationship but it isn't normal to subjugate ourselves to agony. I used to unconsciously think I deserved minimal emotional investment so I would settle for the bare minimum in relationships and it was those times I settled in relationships that left the sting of betrayal against myself.

When I learned God's love I was able to better love myself and I never settled again because I knew what love looked like. Once you learn that you're the daughter of God, you never settle again. After I learned self-love, I was able to really love another human being. God created love to be beautiful and powerful. To know that God loved me despite my flaws made it easier for me to love myself.

When I started to learn my strengths and weaknesses, I was learning to love myself. To learn that God loved me despite my weaknesses taught me that I could also love myself despite my shortcomings. If God thought I was loveable while knowing my secrets, mistakes, regrets, and insecurities, surely I could also accept my humanity. I struggled with a short-temper and I wanted everything to go my way. I thought only my opinions and feelings mattered. That attribute made it difficult for those around me and I thought it made me unlovable. In the Bible, it says God loves his children and when I came to God completely vulnerable about the aspects of myself that I struggled with, God simply replied: "I love you anyway". I think we are looking for that answer from people but humans are flawed. We won't always get that answer from people but it's an answer that God will give you time and time again. I was completely shocked by God's answer. Eventually knowing that God loves you will teach you to love yourself. Here, is a small affirmation that you can say to yourself every day. "I love you, anyway". God says the same thing whether we can accept it or not.

When I didn't love myself you could clearly see the deficit by the ongoing self-criticism in my mind and my dating choices. I would constantly be hard on myself to be perfect. I was so cruel to myself and I didn't think I measured up according to society's standards. Sometimes I didn't think I was pretty enough or smart enough and I settled in relationships.

While I was dating Jake, he didn't have any goals or ambitions. He drank with his friends every weekend and spent all his money on alcohol. He lived at home and I don't remember hearing any plans of him moving out any time soon. I knew I didn't want to marry that kind of man but I stayed with him anyway because I wanted to be connected to someone. I knew he didn't align with my values or morals but still, we had a few things in common. However, all the things we had in common were superficial things that couldn't build a healthy relationship. I knew he wasn't the person that could give me the emotional support, love, and life I wanted.

Truthfully, he and I were connected by our bondage, loneliness, and desperation. He was broken and so was I. Take a mental inventory of your current relationship. Asking yourself these questions. Am I outgrowing this person? Is he verbally abusive? Does he wear me down or build me up? Do I stay with him only because I'm afraid that this is the only chance I'll get at love? Does he have a relationship with God? Is this the person God wants me to spend my life with? Is brokenness and misery enough to go through life together?

These are hard questions to ask yourself in the middle of a relationship. Sometimes we may not want to face the truth and it's easier to ignore the important questions. But if you don't ask these questions, are you just prolonging the inevitable? I'm no longer afraid to ask these questions because I know what I deserve and what God wants for me. I want to encourage you to write down these questions in a journal and listen for God's answers.

I believe that God wants to bless us in every area of our life, especially our romantic life. I don't think God looks down from the heavens and takes comfort in watching us cry over a relationship that He didn't advise us to be in. However, we have free will. So even if we see all the signs that we shouldn't be in that relationship and choose to pursue it anyway; can we really blame God? The signs were clearly there that he wasn't such a great guy but maybe we pursued the relationship anyway. Although God has His hand on our hearts the entire time, the relationship will not work because it isn't in God's will. Even though that wasn't God's choice for us, He will still be there when the relationship ends and He'll help guide us through the heartbreak. He'll help us realize that He was all we needed to begin with.

If I meet a man and there is a lot of work to be done on his values and character, I no longer make it my life's mission to heal him and put him back together again. I'm done with "project relationships". Project relationships are relationships that you see all the red flags but you pursue the relationship anyway. Maybe you're hoping to change him because it'll give you an ego boost and validation that he changed for you. Trust me when I say, you can't change a man who doesn't want to change. When I say change, I don't mean just for a few weeks, I'm talking about a man who is working daily to defeat his bad habits. Meaning you see some long-term results.

If you care about him that much, pray for him but don't settle. You're the only one who loses. Once my broken relationship ended, I realized God could do much more for him than I ever could. If your partner is hurting you emotionally, verbally, or physically I would strongly advise letting go. I can't tell you how many times I've been devastated and disappointed holding onto something God wanted me to let go of. I believe in helping other people but I don't believe God wants us to tolerate disrespect and heartache in our romantic relationship for an ongoing basis. I don't believe you should be overextending yourself for his well-being at the expense of your heart and peace. If I notice a man is getting comfortable mistreating me, degrading me, and disrespecting me it's a done deal now. It's over. I'm not negotiating with someone about how I should be treated in a dating relationship. I've learned to pray over those kinds of people but let God deal with their hearts. I don't need to date them or pursue them romantically. Don't settle for the bare minimum.

It's okay for you to know what you want in a partner and refuse to settle. But you can't be angry at people for not stepping up to be what you want them to be. You can only look in the mirror and ask yourself why you're settling. If a man comes along and he isn't the best fit for you and there are clear indications that he's not what you're looking for, don't date him. If you're in the middle of a relationship and now you feel like you're settling, let go.

If you're single, don't settle and take on a project if he's been unfaithful to other women, he's irresponsible, or disrespectful; it is your responsibility to know you want better for yourself, no matter how attractive he is or desperate you are. No man is fine enough to disrupt your peace or separate you from God.

If you're desperate for love you're going to give the wrong people access to you. Don't settle and utilize all your energy trying to get men to fit the image that you want them to fit. It's better to let go of the relationship than to be desperate for a person who doesn't suit you anyway. It's better to be single than settle for someone who isn't sent by God.

Scripture to Meditate

I will instruct you and teach you in the way you should go;

   I will counsel you with my loving eye on you.

Psalm 32:8

This is what the Lord says—

   your Redeemer, the Holy One of Israel:

"I am the Lord your God,

   who teaches you what is best for you,

   who directs you in the way you should go.

Isaiah 48:17

Settling Prayer

In a Relationship

Heavenly Father, I pray I never settle in a relationship that isn't sent by you. I pray I entertain relationships orchestrated by you and protected by Heaven. I'm currently in a relationship and I feel I'm settling. I pray for the Holy Spirit to guide me. Lord, please give me the discernment to know if I should leave this relationship. I know I'm your daughter and that you love me so I only want what you want for me. I know if I lose this person it's because you have something better in store for me. I pray you cover my heart and protect my spirit. I pray I have the confidence to know I am worth so much more.
In Jesus' name, Amen.

Single

Heavenly Father, I pray I never become so desperate that I step into a relationship that isn't sent by you. I pray I never settle for the bare minimum in my relationship at the expense of losing myself and you. I pray you give me the patience and strength to wait for your best choice for me while single. I pray I seek your love and wisdom during this time. Help me to understand that I don't lack love in my life when I'm loved fiercely by you. Help me to never rush ahead of you and settle.
In Jesus' name, Amen.

CHAPTER TEN

EMBRACE SINGLENESS

There is a time for everything,
and a season for every activity under the heavens:
a time to be born and a time to die,
a time to **plant** and a time to uproot,
a time to kill and a time to **heal**,
a time to **tear down** and a time to **build**,
a time to **weep** and a time to **laugh**,
a time to mourn and a time to dance,
a time to scatter stones and a time to gather them,
a time to embrace and a time to refrain from embracing,
a time to search and a time to give up,
a time to **keep** and a time to **throw away**,
a time to tear and a time to mend,
a time to be silent and a time to speak,
a time to love and a time to hate,
a time for war and a time for peace.

Ecclesiastes 3:1-8

There is a time for everything: a time to be single and a time to be in a relationship. Sometimes we are so preoccupied with getting into a relationship that we bypass singleness because of the shame surrounding being single. Other times we stay in the wrong relationships to avoid being single. Either way, women are fearful of being single but it's during a single-season, God reveals our beauty and worthiness through Him so we won't have to seek validation from a relationship. Developing confidence and worthiness from God is something that others can't take from you. It's during a season of loneliness and desperation that God reveals Himself in mighty ways.

Dating in the 21st century has become so odd because people want to find someone to post photos with on social media. People are searching for other people to be their God and only God can fit that role. We want someone to relieve the sting of loneliness but we end up in relationships that aren't qualified by God. People are carrying so much brokenness around because they're not taking a moment to sit still and listen for God. Rather than wait on God we're running through lovers and it won't relieve the emptiness in our hearts, only God will. God will clearly show us who to date and who to let go of if we ask Him. God doesn't need our help to choose a partner, He is God.

If you're single and you feel like men aren't seeking you be glad because God is keeping you covered. Being single can be such a rewarding time for you and your relationship with Jesus. I want you to know that being single can be such a beautiful time even if it feels like everyone else is in a relationship. Instead of dissecting your insecurities during a single season think of it as a time that the Lord can change your heart and develop you into a woman of God. He can also be protecting you from any unhealthy relationships. I remember while single I would pray:

"Lord, don't bring a man into my life unless he is sent from you. I'm tired of dating carelessly because I keep getting hurt. I'm carrying a lot of brokenness from past relationships and I want to be healed so I can accept the joy you have for me. Men do not decide if I'm worthy and whole. I'm worthy because the Bible says I am. I give this area of my life to you and I'm not going to be consumed by my romantic life. I know that you love me and you're saving your best for me."

Every time I felt the sting of any loneliness, I just repeated this prayer and the lonely feeling would subside because I was putting my faith in God. God was able to use that time to heal my heart from things that I had been hiding from during relationships. I had been running from my childhood, my insecurities, and past heartbreaks.

After my last heartbreak, I was done with dating. I wasn't ready to jump into any new relationship. I didn't want a relationship, situation-ship, messy ex-boyfriend situation; I wanted absolutely nothing to do with dating. I was over men, dating, and the disappointments. I decided to be single for a season and just stay close to God. I devoted myself to my mental, emotional, and physical health. The time I spent alone was such an investment to myself because I learned so much about myself. I learned to keep myself happy and healthy emotionally. I didn't care whether a relationship came into my life because God and I had cultivated so much happiness in my life. I would garden, journal, exercise, travel, and pray. I learned daily how to love myself in a healthy way. My ultimate goal wasn't a relationship and I became content with every aspect of life even without a partner.

I want to explain some of the consequences of not waiting on God and why we should wait for a relationship sent from God. The Bible says, "It's not good for men/women to be alone" meaning that we should be in relationship with others but it doesn't say cry, get cheated on, degrade yourself, lied to, or raise a grown man to get your happily ever after. If a relationship is what you desperately want, I have found that being with the wrong man is worse than being single. Let me say that again, being with the wrong man is worse than being single. Yes, we get the relationship title but at what cost? We also get all the consequences of not waiting on God.

You'll know God wants you to be single when you have no peace about the relationship you're in or it seems as if no one is seeking you. There are times I wish I had stayed single instead of rushing ahead of God because the heartbreak was so bad. There were relationships I had zero peace about but I stayed because I thought I knew better than God about what was best for me. I'd fight with the person about everything and we just didn't make a good match. It felt as if I was trying to put together two puzzle pieces that just didn't fit but I wanted to force it. I was always having a raging war against my partner and I felt no emotional security. I'd either have to plead with him to be responsible or to show me romantic gestures. Or I'd have to push my dreams to the side because I was pouring so much of myself into a relationship that wasn't equally reciprocated. In my heart I knew the relationship wasn't right but I still wanted to be romantically involved with someone.

Trust me when I say that this isn't the relationship that God wants you to be in. If you're wondering why that relationship isn't working the answer is simple, it's because God didn't sign off on that relationship. There could have been some loneliness on your part and you rushed ahead without getting a confirmation from God. I say that with no judgment because I've rushed ahead of God more than a few times. It's important moving forward to ask God for confirmation and feel peace about your relationships.

I want you to take a moment to consider how much of the time you're actually happy in your relationship so you can consider whether to be single again. If you're happy, a majority of the time and have disagreements less than 15% of the time, then we're in the clear. However, if you're frustrated, sad, angry, crying, a significant amount of the time and it is not getting better; it's wise to sit with God and seek His advice about ending the relationship. Know the difference between ongoing emotional abuse and a single disagreement. Usually, instead of ending a relationship, I would drag out the relationship in hopes that it could be salvaged. I was hoping if I kept forgiving that he would change or that he would start to appreciate me. I kept making excuses like "He doesn't know any better or he's been hurt before." When you continue in the wrong relationship there's fighting, verbal abuse, and emotional abuse. Don't wait for God to tell you three times before leaving. The only person you're hurting is yourself. Whether we like it or not God's will, will prevail. Meaning that in the long run, if God doesn't want something to succeed, it won't succeed. God always has something better in mind, it's just a matter of how long you want to continue to hurt and disobey Him.

If you're currently single I want you to know that you're fiercely loved by God and you don't have a deficiency of love in your life. Learn to master being happily single and loving yourself. Use this time to pursue your goals and make memories with loved ones. Don't rush ahead of God and settle for the wrong partner. Being single isn't the worst thing in the world but being in the wrong relationship can feel like the worst thing in the world. Being in a relationship that God doesn't want you to be in means you have to step out of God's will to keep the relationship and it's painful dishonoring God. It's so much better to be single with God than in a relationship separated from God. Embrace being single and don't worry God will love you fiercely during this time. Ask God to fill your heart and pour your love into Him. We are beautiful women created by God and we shouldn't be afraid of being single.

Scripture to Meditate

As for God, His way is perfect; The word of the Lord is proven; He is a shield to all who trust in Him.

Psalms 18:30

Be still and know that I am God,

Psalm 46:10

Prayer

Lord, help me to understand that things don't happen on my timing but yours. Sometimes I rush ahead of you and step outside of your will for my life. Help me to wait on your timing God. I pray I learn to be patient and have faith in your timing. Help me to learn that you love me so much so I don't stay in relationships that aren't ordained by you.

CHAPTER ELEVEN

GOD'S HAND IN HEARTBREAK

After a break-up, know there will be an emptiness in your heart from letting go of that relationship but God will fill that. It will be hard at first to deal with losing someone but the self-love and the relationship you develop with God will make it worth it. It's important to take care of yourself emotionally, spiritually, and mentally during this time and know that it's normal to miss someone but that doesn't mean it's healthy to jump back into that relationship. If God is asking you to let go of a relationship it can either be because the relationship isn't meant to be long-term or God is saving you from anymore heartache. The relationship may not be long-term but every relationship whether good or bad helps us develop character and grow. It's just hard for us to come to terms with the fact that this person's part in our story is over. But if we can change the story in our mind and make it less about an ending and more about a new beginning we can take back our power.

If you want to wallow and pity again tomorrow and the next day and the next day, it's up to you but know that emotions only make up a small portion of the mind. While I admit emotions are important to acknowledge and feel I don't think we should allow them to dictate our entire day, months, or years. Learn to control your thoughts and interrupt them when things are getting dark in your mind. Ask the Lord and angels to cover your mind during your heartache.

I used to let my emotions dictate everything about my life. I would hear a sad song then think of a painful memory. Then that one sad moment would turn into hours of overthinking and replaying memories in my mind. I want you to know that anyone that has left you isn't the person you're meant to spend your life with. I've learned to be okay with that statement. We don't need to go over it in our minds again and again. We just have to accept things for what they currently are and work at moving forward. That is what it means to trust God. You may not have the answer to why something ended but blindly trust that God has something better.

During my walk with God, I was dealing with heartbreak but the weight of sadness became lighter with God every day. Some days I missed him more than others but still every day I took one step toward healing. It did take time to reach a point where I felt completely healed but I got there. I won't say that it was easy but I will say that the woman you become with God will be absolutely worth it. I remember I would tell God in prayer:

"I want to stay single and just focus on you and my purpose. I no longer need a relationship or man to feel whole because I'm whole with you."

I knew God wanted me to stay single for a season and although it was difficult, I knew I was going to be blessed after the season was over. Even when I was in tears hoping for the pain to subside, I knew the God I served would not let me down and He didn't. He won't let you down if you allow Him to heal your heart.

Should we stay friends?

I personally struggled with the "should we be friends" question. I thought maybe me & Jake could be friends because we shared memories together and I didn't want to lose him entirely. During that time apart I thought he would recognize his faults in the relationship and sharpen up but that's not what happened. Instead, I was filled with confusion because I was still allowing him access to my life but I knew we couldn't continue in the relationship because we had grown apart. The gray area after the break-up was because of my own decision not to obey God and let the relationship go.

I had to learn the hard way that entertaining an ex allowed the devil an open door into my life and it kept my mind clouded with confusion. I have learned that exes shouldn't be kept on social media or kept in contact with after a break-up. The devil can use that as a tool to keep you attached to your past and bondage. If God asks you to put a relationship down, put it down.

Be alert and of sober mind. Your enemy the devil prowls around like a roaring lion looking for someone to devour.

1 Peter 5:8

I wanted to have control over the situations in my life and I thought I knew better than God. I thought I could manage my feelings and keep old boyfriends around even when God told me not to. I ended up in a position where I was hurt and confused all the time because I couldn't define the relationship. In the end, I learned to cut ties, pray over ex-boyfriends, and let them go. When God asks you to let someone go, don't fight with Him. He can see further ahead in the future than you can. That unhealthy relationship He's asking you to let go of could have been your destruction. The relationship can also be something sent from the devil to keep you in depression and pain for years to come. God works things together for your good and He is probably saving you from a lifetime of heartache. These questions may come to your mind:

- "What if he's the one?"
- "What if he starts to get better? "
- "What if he starts dating someone else?"
- "What if he changes?"
- "What if we end up together in a few years?"

When the "what if" thoughts start to come to mind, don't entertain them. What if he isn't the one and you spent all this time away from the actual person God really has for you? What if he never changes? Would you be okay with the way he treats you and his habits for the rest of your life?

After the break-up don't live in a fantasy and only glorify the good moments; remember the reasons the relationship didn't work and the painful moments. Don't fool yourself by remembering only the good things. After a break-up, we have selective memory and choose to only remember the good things. Remind yourself that God wants a better quality of life for you if that relationship wasn't healthy. Sometimes we just grow apart from others and that's okay too. If the relationship has reached its limitation, then honor the limitation. God designed it to end but something better is coming. God is not the type of God that will make you suffer without giving you something better. It's cliché but it's true. You will be restored and you will be blessed after letting go of what God asked you to let go of. God believes in you and He knows you can get through this storm. Your obedience will show God you trust him. In return, He will show you the relationship you loved so much was actually the destruction of your peace.

After your season of suffering, God in all His grace will restore, confirm, strengthen and establish you.

1 Peter 5:10

Whether you let go of a relationship or someone else ends the relationship, it will hurt. Losing someone hurts. There will be many tears and you will question whether this was the right decision, but I can tell you that anything God asks you to do is the right decision. Press into God every moment of this season or you will search the world for something to fill your emptiness. You may go into bars or clubs and think drinking will help you forget but the heartache will still be there in the morning. There is nowhere you can run to escape the heartache, so face it with God. Sit there and cry to God. Tell Him how hurt and disappointed you are. Explain to Him your frustration and how you think He let you down. Be vulnerable during this time and you'll find out God cares more than anyone.

Once the tears start to subside God will give you a little more strength each day to move forward. When you feel anxiety or sadness come into your heart, immediately flee into the arms of God. Grab your Bible or listen to a sermon about strength. The Bible says the devil is like a lion roaring around looking for someone who is in a weakened state so he can attack their mind. When we are going through a break-up, we are extremely vulnerable. Press into God and stay under His arms during this time.

Grief, loss, and disappointment is a part of life. It's nearly impossible to go through life without a loss or disappointment but we can learn to manage our response to those parts of life. Sometimes we will want to keep a relationship more than anything but God will say, "I love you too much to see you hurt all the time, I have something new for you."

See, I am doing a new thing! Now it springs up; do you not perceive it? I am making a way in the wilderness and streams in the wasteland.
Isaiah 43:19

I have gone through enough storms in life to tell you that you will make it through. You will start to smile and laugh again because you will find new love, God's love. The kind of love that can't be taken. Even when we lose someone we don't lose God's love. His love isn't dependent on our status, wealth, beauty, or external circumstances. Even if the person you love most abandons you, God will never abandon you. If the other person breaks up with you it can be extremely difficult and it may feel like God isn't around during this time but I can assure you He is. Don't be afraid of the ending of a relationship because God will be there to sustain you and uplift your heart when you let go of that person.

There will be times you think of him and miss him but just pray. A prayer can do much more for the person than you can physically, by entering back into a relationship that wasn't healthy in the first place. After the prayer, lift your head, get up and continue to follow God. The woman you've always wanted to be and your purpose is waiting for you to show up. Everything will start to come together, just one step at a time. Ending a relationship isn't the end, it's the beginning.

When I decided to stop hunting down relationships I could see what God was trying to do in my life. God was trying to get me alone to heal my hurt and reveal His purpose for my life. When I was in these relationships I was so focused on building the other person and maintaining the relationship that I couldn't focus where God wanted me to focus.

God wanted to heal my heart. There were some wounds in my childhood that needed to be healed and I had been carrying a broken heart from past relationships. I had also been carrying insecurity, inferiority, and jealousy. There is a time to tear down and a time to build. I started to tear down the insecure girl and God revealed the woman He had always designed me to be.

Now, when I'm in the middle of a single season it isn't dreadful. My whole perspective on single season has changed drastically. On a trip to Europe, I heard my friend, Stephanie, say she was happily single while discussing her relationship status. I love it and I think it's a statement we should take ownership of while single. Amazed by what she said it made me think about how much more happy I was being single than I had been a year earlier in an unhappy relationship with the wrong person.

If you feel discouraged about your singleness while looking at social media ask yourself, how many of those relationships are healthy? We really couldn't say because the truth is we don't know. When we're going through a break-up, we assume everyone else is happy. Social media doesn't give us the truth about the relationships around us. We only see a few photos into their lives and they pick the best photos. How many of them settled because they were desperate? How many people are really with their soulmate? How many of those people are fighting or arguing every night? We don't know, nor is our concern. We have to be smart enough to know that we may not be seeing the whole truth on social media. We don't want to make a desperate decision to jump into a relationship just so we can sell our happiness on social media. I'm not a pessimist, some people may be in healthy relationships designed by God and we should rejoice for them but we shouldn't use social media as a pressure to jump into the wrong relationships after a break-up.

While I was going through a heartbreak I started a garden and every day I poured my love into the garden. It may seem silly but my roses were flourishing and so was I. At the same time I had so many loved ones and friends that were praying over me and supporting me during this time. One Sunday as I was in tears, my grandma grabbed my hand and assured me that everything would be okay. As I looked in her eyes, I felt just how much she loved me and it finally became clear that my life was filled with love. I was unlimited in how many loving experiences I could have in my life when my heart was open to sources around me.

Another time I felt deep love from God was while sitting in a local garden alone. I looked at the flowers blooming and I realized how much love God had poured into the flowers in the garden. If God had poured that much love into flowers than surely he had poured that much love into me. I learned to find love in the smallest of moments and that is when I realized that losing someone didn't mean that I wasn't loved by God. It meant that God loved me so much He wanted much more for me than what I was getting from those relationships.

God loves you unconditionally so He will cover your heart. Practice welcoming different loving experiences into your life. I want to remind you that you don't have a deficit for love in your life. Consistently pursue God for healing and wisdom. Pray and ask God to stop replaying old memories in your mind. Ask Him to teach you mental discipline. When I started to love myself and discipline my mind, I was able to heal. Now I'm not threatened by someone walking away because I know exactly who I am in Christ. I am spiritually disciplined and I take care of my emotional health. I am following my dreams and I know for a fact that God will bring the right person for me to create a life with. I am not desperately searching for a man but instead, I choose to develop my character as a woman and build a relationship with Jesus.

Scripture to Meditate

When you go through deep waters, I will be with you. When you go through rivers of difficulty, you will not drown.
Isaiah 43:2

I love those who love me, and those who seek me find me
Proverbs 8:17

The Lord will guide you always; he will satisfy your needs in a sun-scorched land and will strengthen your frame. You will be like a well-watered garden, like a spring whose waters never fail.
Isaiah 58:11

He will wipe away every tear from their eyes, and death shall be no more, neither shall there be mourning, nor crying, nor pain anymore, for the former things have passed away.
Revelation 21:4

Yet you, LORD, are our Father. We are the clay, you are the potter; we are all the work of your hand.
For you created my inmost being; you knit me together in my mother's womb.
Psalm 139:13

Prayer

Lord, I'm heartbroken and defeated. Help me to press into you during this time. Don't let me run to the world to heal my heart. I pray I don't return to relationships you've asked me to let go of. I pray I heal from this heartbreak and trust you during this difficult time. I will put my faith in you and not in my fear of loneliness. I pray I use this time to get closer to you Lord. Amen.

CHAPTER TWELVE

WHO DOES GOD WANT US TO DATE?

When our hearts are healed and we decide to start dating again we should absolutely have new criteria for the men we want to start a relationship with. When I started dating again I wanted to date a man who knew the word of God and had a prayer life. I knew I wanted God to be the center of my next relationship, if not it wasn't worth pursuing. God was going to be the solid foundation of my romantic life because I had already done all my relationships without God and saw them fall apart. Moving forward I didn't want to have any relationship that God didn't bless.

When I started seeing a new guy who I met at church. I paid attention to everything and I wasn't living in fantasy as I had before. I wasn't just inventing qualities that weren't there or falling for someone's potential; I was truly evaluating the person in front of me. This guy always showed up on time for our dates and always made it a point to text me back even if he was busy. He didn't leave me on read for days or weeks. He was not playing games. From the beginning, I knew where I stood with him. If we as women are parading around saying we're grown women then we should not tolerate game playing from any man, no matter how handsome he is.

Another sign this man prioritized was he was attentive to my emotional needs and patient with my schedule. He planned dates and the only thing I had to worry about was which dress to wear. He reminded me verbally and showed me with actions just how much I meant to him. I never questioned his intentions. I never had to ask him to make me a priority, I knew I mattered by his actions. I never questioned where we stood because he always made it clear with his actions that I was important in his life. I loved that he was a complete gentleman and not just for the first few weeks or months but regularly.

He proved to me that he was the real deal so I gave him my time. It wasn't just his actions that were attractive but it was also his internal qualities that were just as beautiful. He was ambitious, kind, understanding, compassionate, and he loved to work. I had always told God I wanted to spend my life standing next to a man who I could be proud to stand next to. Spending time with him was so easy. I was used to guarding my heart by any means necessary and when I went into a relationship I was usually fearful and defensive but that wasn't the case with him. I regularly asked God about him and God kept giving me a word that I was in the right relationship.

This man treated me exactly how I imagined God thought I deserved to be treated. He always spoke to me with respect and boasted to our mutual friends about me. It was clear that he wasn't in lust but he actually saw me. I had heard about men who went to church but still acted like the kind of man that you'd meet at the bar so I was diligent to pay attention to everything about him because I wanted to be sure I wasn't entering another toxic or codependent relationship.

I prayed regularly to make sure that both of us were honoring God with our relationship. Everything with him seemed to fit and we complimented each other very well. We laughed and always spoke to each other with respect. In my old relationships, I was used to yelling and arguing with the other person which was draining. With this relationship, we always checked in with each other to make sure our emotional and communication needs were being met. I could tell this was different than anything I had ever experienced before. I could tell God was in it and I'm still in this relationship. Whether or not we will marry is something I will continue to pray about. A man could be absolutely amazing but you still need a word from God.

When you start dating again make sure that God is leading you into the relationship. Make sure both of you feel the same and are on the same page. Don't be afraid to ask the other person's intentions. If you have to compete for his attention with other women that's not the man God has for you. God isn't going to ask you to be in a relationship where you have to chase and pursue a man who isn't chasing and pursuing you. If at some point along the way you forget what you deserve, here is a shortlist of qualities we should be looking for in men.

QUALITIES WE SHOULD BE EVALUATING IN A MAN

- ## He has a relationship with God

If he doesn't have a relationship with God, how can he have a relationship with you? If he doesn't know God's love, how can he love you? What moral and value system is he following? If he is following the world's example, then guess what the world is teaching him? It's teaching to give in to lust and flesh.

- ## He demonstrates kindness with his words (no ulterior motives)

A man who is kind to you is much better than a man who is constantly hurting you verbally and emotionally. That may seem like an obvious statement but many of us go through the bad boy phase. We only give our heart to the man who treats us poorly and ignores us. There is nothing romantic about a man who isn't kind or compassionate.

Also, it's important to guard your heart against men who are kind only because they want something in return. There are men who are kind because they want sex. They use kind words and wait for a woman to put her guard down just to get her vulnerable to sleep with him. When you're a confident woman in God you know you have much more to offer than just sex so don't think you need to give a man sex to be worthy or keep him. **Trust me you don't have to dishonor God to get the man God wants you to be with.** Time to grow up, bad boys may be cute on the outside but they're not who we want to build a life with or have children with.

- **Sensitive and vulnerable**

A man who doesn't dismiss your feelings is a man worth keeping. Pay attention to whether he can be delicate with your feelings. Being sensitive is a manly trait. It takes courage to go against society and be sensitive in a world that tells men they can't be sensitive. Women have continuously praised men that dismiss the needs and feelings of women. I don't know about you but I don't want to spend forever with a man who dismisses my feelings and can't be sensitive to my emotional needs. A man who is sensitive to your needs emotionally and mentally is attractive.

- **He respects you**

A man should always treat you with the utmost respect. No more giving attention to men who disrespect us or waste our time. He respects you with his words and actions. A man that respects you, respects your time, space, and energy. He calls back, he texts back, he lets you know he is busy. A man that respects you doesn't go ghost on you for weeks. He also doesn't disrespect you in front of others. **If he doesn't respect your time or space. Don't give him yours.**

- **He cares about your feelings**

If he is <u>consistently</u> hurting your feelings, even after you've told him your emotional triggers it's because he doesn't care about your feelings. A man who cares will see that something hurts you and refrain from doing it again. If he cares about your feelings trust me he wants to avoid hurting them. A man who has a relationship with God will want to cover you and protect your heart. When you're getting to know him and

121

you notice right away he's inconsiderate and doesn't care about your feelings, it's going to be a painful road ahead. Save yourself the heartache and don't give this type of man the time of day. You can't force someone to care about your feelings and you should never be okay with someone hurting you.

- **He is responsible.**

When we're young we make some unnecessary choices. We think the bad boy persona is attractive and when you mature you realize it's not cute to nag a man to be responsible, spend his money wisely, and chase ambition. It's a headache and unnecessary. If he is out drinking every weekend, in strip-clubs or can't maintain a job, that's a red flag.

Similarly, urge young men to be sensible and self-controlled and to behave wisely.
Titus 2:6

Pay attention to his life and his actions and what he puts his energy into. If he just talks about starting a business but never takes action to get a business license and just sits at home twiddling his thumbs and hanging with his boys, there's your proof he's all talk and no action. A man that is disciplined with his work, his goals, and his character development, now that's attractive. I've heard so many women tell me stories about them supporting men financially and that's a red flag. This isn't about being materialistic if he doesn't like to work and can't hold down a job, that's a clear sign he's not responsible and it's not your job to teach him to be responsible so he can be the man of your dreams. Ambition is attractive and a man that knows where he is going next, that's a man worth dating. A man that is responsible is someone who can lead you through life in a relationship. The dynamics between men and women in a romantic relationship was never meant to be a mother-son relationship. You're not his mommy you're a grown woman so wait for a grown man.

RED FLAGS

- **An enemy to God**

    If a man doesn't have a relationship with God, how can he begin to have a relationship with you? If he can't be vulnerable with God, how can he be vulnerable with you? If he isn't sensitive to the Holy Spirit how can be sensitive with you? If he doesn't have God as a spiritual anchor, what grounds him? Who is teaching him his morals and values? Is he following society? Does he think sleeping with multiple women makes him a man? Does he think strip clubs, drugs and drinking makes him a man? A man who doesn't know God is a red flag. He is a man that can be easily tempted and has no spiritual discipline.

- **Womanizer**

    The man with the wandering eye. A man that is always chasing different women or known for cheating is a huge red flag. Please don't go into this situation thinking you can change him and get some internal validation from tying him down. Pray to God for discernment to see men for who they really are and not for what you wish them to be. Don't fall just for potential because you have no real evidence they have the desire to change. The risk isn't worth a heartache or getting cheated on.

- **Temper**

A man that can't control his temper. A man that fights with you or gets angry very quickly, not a good sign. It's not attractive at all because if you're hoping to go long term with someone remember your children will pick up habits from the man you're dating. If you wouldn't want your son to turn out just like him why would you date him? Remember when you're dating you're picking someone to tackle life with and demonstrate love to your children. Easily angered is not something you want to live with for the rest of your life nor is it something you want your children to grow up witnessing.

- **Struggles with alcohol and drugs.**

Someone who struggles with alcohol or drugs is someone who is struggling with something deeper. From the beginning, if you see these signs don't hope that you can convert him for romantic purposes because he may drag you down into the darkness with him. Pray for him but don't start a romantic relationship with him. **Don't be tempted by darkness.** Are you willing to risk your heart or a potential soul tie?

Man or God first?

Whether you're single or in a relationship, your first relationship should be with God. Take it from someone who has used everything but God to fill a void, it doesn't work if you don't put God first. God isn't a second choice. I don't want to arrive at Heaven and have God say, "You always put men before me." If you're already in a relationship I recommend you have a strong foundation with God first. If you're single, don't make it your whole life mission to chase down men to love you.

If you're single when you come together with another person and he has a good foundation in God you'll both have a strong foundation in the Lord and be covered by Heaven. The people we decide to date can lead us into destruction so we should always put our relationship with God first. If we are connected to God then we have much more clarity about the people in our lives and whether those people should stay in our lives. God is the only one that can be with us with every single second of our life until the day we die. Our relationship with Him should be the most important. If you count on others to be your God it holds others to an unrealistic standard and keeps you apart from God.

Here are some examples of how we put men first even if we're single. If we spend all day thinking about them and how to catch them, then we're putting men before God. Sometimes we fall in love with a man we've created in our mind and I personally struggled with this. Any man that would come into my life I would have this idea of who I wanted him to be and what I wanted him to act like. I'd spent a significant amount of time either nagging him to be what I wanted him to be or meeting new men.

It's exhausting only worrying about men. I wanted love so badly that when men came into my life and wanted a chance, I would try to condition them to fit my projection. Let me tell you this is A LOT of work. Trying to force someone to be who they are not or forcing someone to do romantic things that they just don't want to do is exhausting. Why force someone to be what they aren't? You're going to spend years training him to be the man you envisioned in your mind? It's not fair to another person and it's a lot of work for me just to have the relationship fall apart anyway.

I've found that it's much easier to let go of putting men first. If you put God first, he'll answer all your other prayers.

Scripture to Meditate

You shall love the Lord your God with all your heart and with **all** your soul and with **all** your mind. This is the great and first commandment. And a second is like it: You shall love your neighbor as yourself. On these two commandments depend all the Law and the Prophets.

Matthew 22:37-40

You shall have no other gods before me.

Exodus 20:3

Prayer

Lord, above all I pray to put you first in my life. I don't want to put my career, friends, or others before you. Help me to love you fiercely God and put my faith in you. Help me to prioritize my relationship with you and give you glory. In Jesus' name, amen.

CHAPTER THIRTEEN

VALIDATED THROUGH SOCIAL MEDIA OR GOD?

I fear for women who have grown to value social media so much that they use social media as a daily tool to measure their worth. I look at my younger cousins and I think they are absolutely beautiful inside and out. They are kind, giving, intellectual, and love God; yet they look to social media and feel they are lacking in some way. There are women that measure their worth by following the lives of random people on social media. Some people on social media project a fake image of confidence but have no real root in confidence. They use likes and comments as a way to affirm their worthiness and beauty; yet feel empty and unworthy on the inside. Having a relationship with God has helped me to overflow with beauty and develop confidence. I have found that having a relationship with God is the secret to being a confident woman.

It is difficult for women to cultivate self-love when everything in society tells them they are unlovable. Body dysmorphia, insecurity, and self-rejection are so prevalent in society and that is why we should look to God to root our confidence and not to the world. There is no surgery, lip filler, or implant that can change the soul of a woman. The opinions and trends of society are constantly changing but the word of God doesn't change. When I first started my walk with the Lord, the Holy Spirit showed me that I was putting all my worth in the opinions of others. Specifically, that I was using social media to affirm my worthiness and beauty.

At the beginning of my walk with God, I started to make it a habit to delete social media for a short time to keep myself close to God. I didn't allow the devil to use social media to sway the work that God was doing in my life. Since I was just starting my journey I didn't want to let the enemy use other women to dictate how I felt about myself. If I started to notice that the enemy was using social media as a way to spark negative thoughts, I'd cast the thoughts down immediately. I would reject any insecure thoughts and reclaim what the Bible said about me. I'd repeat, "I am whole in Jesus Christ."

Even now I take a break from social media sometimes and it gives me a chance to get reacquainted with myself and God. I believe that social media can sometimes be a tool used by the devil to keep us unsatisfied with our lives and the way we look. Social media can also be a tool to spread light, love, and the gospel. It is up to be diligent to protect our hearts and have discernment.

There is so much being poured into our minds without conscious regulation while on social media. Our minds are such a beautiful place and we must be conscious of what we allow to come into our minds and hearts. If the women we are following on social media are selling a certain body image, a thought may pass through our minds "I don't look like these women. That is what beauty looks like." Then we may look in the mirror and realize we don't fit that image and it may affect our overall sense of worth. Some influencers and celebrities are selling products and a body image that reinforces insecurity. I don't believe all of them are doing it intentionally, I think they are just recycling their own insecurities.

For the purpose of this book, I want to teach you to find your worth in God, not in other people or what they think of you. Since we're learning to build a relationship with Jesus we can learn that we're whole and we're beautiful because God said so. We should disconnect with social media for a while and seek God for our likes and comments. We don't need validation from our followers because we are valued and affirmed by God, the Creator of the universe. If you've ever been to a pottery class or worked on a project you know it takes focus and time to create a work of art. Each of us are God's individual work of art. We each have our own special gifts, talents, and purpose. We each have our own beauty and authenticity and there is no need to yearn to look like anyone else. Each woman is a work of art that God poured his love into.

Yet you, LORD, are our Father. We are the clay, you are the potter;
we are all the work of your hand.
Isaiah 64:8

Whenever I'm tempted to compare myself to other women whether it's someone in person or on social media I remember that I'm whole in Jesus Christ. During those insecure moments, I would just repeat to myself, "I'm beautiful and the beauty of other women doesn't take away from the fact that I'm also beautiful."

One night I was praying and I heard God say, "You are beautiful and worthy to me." I had just been scrolling on social media and while I was praying He said: "Don't let those people fool you or make you feel dissatisfied with your life." God doesn't look at the external He looks at the heart. When I feel tempted to judge my worth based on my circumstances or beauty I remember to seek out God and see what the Bible says about what worthiness means to God. If you're struggling with good things to say about yourself just look in the Bible because it has so many good things to say about us.

Instead of using external validation as a measure for beauty I now measure my worth based on the fact that Jesus died for me. He thought I was worthy enough to die for. In that statement alone I know that I'm worthy to God so I don't need affirmation from men or people. When you feel compelled to measure your beauty remember that you are beautiful to Jesus Christ. We should aspire to be beautiful to God not beautiful to the world. Being beautiful to God is much more important than being beautiful for social media. Don't measure your beauty based on your waist size but measure your beauty based on the fruit of the Spirit that you demonstrate in your daily life. God thinks you're beautiful whenyou praise Him and demonstrate kindness and love to strangers. God rejoices when He can see your kind heart and empathy. That is truly a good measure of beauty.

If anyone has ever made a negative comment regarding your beauty or weight decide to give that comment to God to heal. Do not dwell on the opinions of others, dwell on God's word. The enemy could have used that person's negative comment to control your mind with insecurity. Don't give the enemy power over your mind. See yourself through God's eyes and make the darkness tremble with your God-given confidence.

Now that I've grown in my confidence, I measure my beauty by how many acts of love and kindness I can demonstrate per day. I know that God delights when I pray and cover other people. During prayer, I want to open doors for people who are struggling with emotional pain and I know that is something about me that is beautiful to God. Brand name purses and shoes don't impress God. My love for Him and my love for others impresses Him.

Once you feel beautiful on the inside, beauty begins to emulate outward. I enjoy getting ready and putting on make-up because it makes me feel good but I don't use make-up and clothes as a measurement of worthiness. I also want to note that it's completely okay to enjoy dressing up but in the eyes of God, He is much more concerned with what is dwelling on the inside of our hearts. I know God is dwelling on the inside of me so when I step outside wearing make-up and my hair is done it isn't just some superficial cover-up for confidence because God is in my heart. Women who walk with the Lord have confidence. And our worthiness is deeper than just our external beauty.

In your journal I want you to write beauty affirmations to yourself and I want you to search for scriptures in the Bible that refer to beauty. Repeat them in the car or at work. When you're struggling with insecurity or feelings of unworthiness repeat the affirmations to yourself. Don't let the spirit of insecurity dictate your mind and tell you that you aren't beautiful because that isn't true. God would never say that to you so learn to distinguish the thoughts in your mind and where they're coming from. Dark spirits will try to get you to dwell on negative thoughts, but Jesus will whisper positive things. Learn to cast down negative thoughts and repeat the positive words that Jesus says to you.

Scripture to Meditate

Your beauty should not come from outward adornment, such as elaborate hairstyles and the wearing of gold jewelry or fine clothes. Rather, it should be that of your inner self, the unfading beauty of a gentle and quiet spirit, which is of great worth in God's sight.
1 Peter 3:3-4

You are altogether beautiful, my darling; there is no flaw in you.
Song of Songs 4:7

I praise you because I am fearfully and wonderfully made;
your works are wonderful,
I know that full well.
Psalm 139:14

But the LORD said to Samuel, "Do not consider his appearance or his height, for I have rejected him. The LORD does not look at the things people look at. People look at the outward appearance, but the LORD looks at the heart.
1 Samuel 16:7

I also want the women to dress modestly, with decency and propriety, adorning themselves, not with elaborate hairstyles or gold or pearls or expensive clothes, but with good deeds, appropriate for women who profess to worship God.
1 Timothy 2:9-10

Prayer

Lord, I pray I put my worth in you alone. I pray I see myself through your eyes and not the eyes of the world. I pray I don't try to be who social media tells me I should be. I pray I don't follow women who aren't in alignment with you God. I pray I don't value the opinions of strangers rather than yours. Help me to build my confidence in you and not the opinions of those who don't have a relationship with you God. Help me know that I'm your beautiful daughter.

In Jesus' name, amen.

CHAPTER FOURTEEN

WHY ISN'T GOD BLESSING ME?

It's easy to become envious of others when we feel that God is blessing everyone but us. There can be feelings of inadequacy that linger after seeing graduation pics, engagement photos, pregnancy announcements, and career advancements for others. I have learned over time not to envy others because of their blessings because my time will come and so will yours. God wants to bless each of us but there is an appointed time for all of us. If we can come to terms with the fact that God wants to bless us and He will bless us, we won't be envious of others. It will also teach us not to worry about our human timelines because we'll know for a fact that our blessing is coming. In the meantime, we can just enjoy all the small beautiful moments that life has to offer us.

We are God's children and He doesn't run out of magic moments for all of us so we shouldn't have hearts filled with envy against our sisters receiving their magic moments. I struggled with jealousy for a long time because it felt like God had forgotten me. It seemed like everyone else was moving ahead in life and nothing new was happening for me. When couples posted photos of their engagements or baby shower I wondered when it would be my time.

After college, my colleagues were striving for their next degree and I began to wonder when God would help me get into graduate school or help me advance in my career. I wondered when I would get married or start a family. Although I planned to wait to be married and have a child I'd still hear the enemy whisper "Those women are the same age as you and they're starting families or they're the same age as you and advancing in their career." My heart would fill with insecurity and jealousy. Later I found out that those women admired me for pursuing a college degree and waiting to start a family. Those classmates that I was envious of felt they were striving for master's degrees in a field they weren't passionate about. God is so intentional about blessing us with a season of waiting or a season of working. A season of waiting can be a blessing because it can prepare us for the next season of life when God decides to give us the acceptance letter to the school, give us the promotion, or give us marriage.

It is important to honor where God wants us to be. If you are in college or if you're a mother, God has placed you in that position for a reason. If you haven't gotten a promotion or been accepted to school yet, just wait on God. Trust me when I say you don't want any plan not backed up by Heaven. If you go ahead of God, trust me you will come against doors that will not open. If you're within God's timing for your life, God will open all the doors. God created each of us with a special assignment for our life and a specific timeline for our life. Don't lose hope or be discouraged by comparing to the lives of others. Just focus on your path and honor the beauty of what God is doing in your life right now. If it seems like nothing new is happening, enjoy the stillness of life because things will pick up again. If God is asking you to wait, then wait. If God is putting you in a position to work, then work.

I am committed to mastering myself and enjoying all the different seasons of life. I've learned to enjoy where God has called me to be and not spend my entire life comparing my life to other women. You don't want to wake up one day and realize you let go of all the small beautiful moments God had to offer, comparing your life to someone else. Don't look to the right or to the left to compare with other women, just look forward to the doors God is opening for you. Climbing up the success ladder also doesn't mean we've made it in the eyes of God. You could have a degree or be the CEO of a company and that doesn't mean you've honored God along the way. While you're striving for a career, children, or husband, remember to continue seeking Jesus. What is the point of getting everything you ever wanted but forfeit your soul?

And what do you benefit if you gain the whole world but lose your own soul? Is anything worth more than your soul?
Matthew 16:26

It helps that I have learned to be secure in who God has called me to be or I would be comparing myself to other women all the time. It has taken some time to own who I am and sometimes I still might have the thought "Are you good enough?" Satan tries to intimidate me all the time with these kinds of thoughts, but I serve a God that knows that I'm strong enough to carry out his work. So when a thought like that comes to my mind I make sure to dismiss it. My answer to those mental attacks will always be:

"My God has made me beautiful and He will fulfill His promises to me. I am enough for God and I will not envy others."

Whether it be financially, career-wise, family, marriage, or education God will come through for you. If you entertain negative thoughts you will become chained to the idea that you're not good enough or that God will never bless you. I know with full confidence that God has an appointed time for every event in your life. God thinks you're absolutely beautiful and valuable so don't compare yourself to anyone or yearn for the lives of others when God has made your life just as beautiful. Expect blessings. Here are scriptures to remind you that you are beautiful and set apart:

I am a beautiful creation of God
Psalm 139:14

I am complete with Christ
Colossians 2:10

I am loved with an everlasting Love
Jeremiah 31:3

God holds my hand
Isaiah 41:13

God takes great delight in you
Zephaniah 3:17

I want to encourage you to love the women in your lives and always cheer them on. God will cheer for you and slip you some blessings as you cheer for them.

If there is ever a case of jealousy remember that God loves you and has wonderful plans for you despite what your timeline looks like. Pray that God removes the jealousy from your heart. I would also encourage you to pray for the other woman so that the enemy doesn't have a chance to poison your heart. Just because someone else is achieving their dream right now doesn't mean that God won't fulfill His promise to you. We can all get there. I no longer look to the side of me to see whether another woman has more blessings than me. I am just looking ahead, waiting on God. I have much more peace just focusing on the beautiful gifts God has given me and you should take some time to think of the beautiful gifts God has given you.

Scripture to Meditate

Let your eyes look straight ahead; fix your gaze directly before you.
Give careful thought to the paths for your feet and be steadfast in all
your ways.
Do not turn to the right or the left; keep your foot from evil.
Proverbs 4:25-27

Carry each other's burdens, and in this way you will fulfill the law of
Christ.
Galatians 6:2

One who has unreliable friends soon comes to ruin, but there is a friend
who sticks closer than a brother.
Proverbs 18:24

Prayer

Lord, I pray you remove any jealousy from my heart. I pray you remove jealousy so I don't stay separated from you God. I pray that I can cheer on my fellow brothers and sisters in Christ. I am waiting for an abundance of blessings to come in life. I will enjoy the beauty in everyday life. I will enjoy the laugh of a loved one, beauty in nature, and moments that bring me joy.

CHAPTER FIFTEEN

LEAVING UNHEALTHY FRIENDSHIPS

Friendships are very important and God wants us to be mindful of who we're friends with. Friends can lead us into destruction just like bad relationships can. The enemy can place a discouraging, jealous, God-hating woman in your life and you'll mistakenly call her friend. She may not say she hates God but if she's encouraging you to disobey God then that is not a godly friendship.

A good friend encourages you, uplifts you, and pushes you to God. Good friends don't disrespect you or cross your emotional boundaries. They don't talk badly about you or hope you fail because of jealousy stored in their hearts. They aren't leading you into self-destruction or darkness. Take an inventory of the top five people you spend time with. Evaluate whether they build you up or tear you down.

Sometimes God will ask us to take a step back from a friendship for a season and other times He will completely remove a friendship. One time my childhood friend Jacky was having a difficult year. I kept praying that she would reach for the Lord because I knew how badly she was struggling emotionally. She wasn't making the best decisions as a result of her emotional wounds and I was worried about her well-being. However, despite my love for her as a friend, I couldn't join her at bars because the Lord was still working in my heart. I was in a position where I was still vulnerable to return to my old ways so I kept my distance. It was hard to watch her struggle but I prayed and prayed for her. A year later she came to Lord and she gave her heart to God. Prayer is so powerful even if you can't physically be in someone's life.

My other best friend Angie was also able to submit to God. She was in a relationship that God was prompting her to let go of and drinking often. During her relationship we didn't speak much. Although we hadn't spent much time together or spoken much during that time, I still considered her a best friend. She would randomly call me and express her doubts about that relationship. I remember thinking to myself that God was going to end that relationship once she was ready. After praying for her and her own soul work, she submitted to God's will. She graduated from nursing school and a few months later we moved in together. After some time of living together, the Lord began to work in her heart and transform her life. She started to make decisions that were aligned with God's will for her life and she was able to have the strength to let go of that relationship that lasted several years. Now she is devoted to God and expresses her gratitude to Him daily and the three of us can support each other with godly wisdom. We give each other advice to press into God as opposed to suggesting that we drink to solve our issues. God has the power to transform your friendships so I encourage you to seek God about the people you really care about and pray for their healing. I also want you to know that it's okay to take a season apart to let God work in their lives and when the time is right God will bring you back together if it's in His will.

God will also ask you to release friendships that will not help you grow and prosper. Some people aren't meant to stay in your life and it's wise to let those friendships go. I once had a friend who I'll call Jane and I thought I could consider her a real friend until the Lord showed me otherwise. Her lifestyle would suggest that drinking, drugs, and having sex with different men was the way to have fun. Looking back I can see that the devil had direct access to my heart through this friend who was an influence on me. The only time we would hang out was to drink and party. Jane was self-absorbed and she only cared about how many people were following her on social media. She would refer to other women as "peasants" to inflame her ego and insecurities. I began to see the kind of thoughts stored in her heart as soon as I started my relationship with God. I also realized that if she had been gossiping to me about other people surely she was gossiping about me to others. This friendship soon ended as I started walking with the Lord and He prompted me to pray for her but stay away from her. Although I was disappointed that I couldn't keep her in my life God brought me new fulfilling friendships.

When I started making friends at church I noticed the women God led me to be friends with didn't gossip and whenever I talked about a new accomplishment, they rejoiced. Growing up I was accustomed to women being jealous or discouraging about my dreams. These women at church were committed to helping others emotionally and serving God's kingdom. They wanted to help others find God and now I want to do the same for the women around me. I never felt an ounce of doubt when it came to their intentions or their friendship. They were so beautiful in spirit. Although I had a great experience meeting these women at church please know that even in church, you should have discernment about the people you're allowing to pour into your life. Women at church can still be gossiping and have ill intentions. The Bible says to be diligent about the friends you spend time with so listen to the words stored up in their hearts and listen for God's approval.

As iron sharpens iron, so one man sharpens another.
Proverbs 27:17

The foundations I had from my past friendships were built on gossip and being self-destructive. I was used to sitting around with friends wallowing in self-pity, gossiping, and talking about how terrible our relationships were. At the time I thought that this was the foundation for a good friendship but at church, I learned what a real friendship really looked like.

My outlook on friendships has drastically changed over the years. The friends I have in my life now are beautiful and I love to celebrate them. Many of my friends have healed from childhood wounds, abusive relationships, and insecurities. I celebrate their internal healing and any advancements in their careers. Whenever they struggle in life I am there to pray over them. They support my dreams and I support them, and we encourage each other in every season of life. There is no space for jealousy because we're all running the race of life with God's hand on us. We aren't trying to outshine each other; we are just trying to love each other fiercely.

A true friend is someone who wants to see the best for you and pushes you toward God. These people at church never claimed to be perfect but they did their best to reflect Jesus. They were humble about the times they fell short in life and it made them empathize with those starting their journey with the Lord. They did their best to be kind, to forgive, and were slow to anger. I knew that was the kind of person I wanted to become and that's why I wanted to spend more time with them. They pushed me to be better. They also held me accountable to make sure I was staying close to God which I needed as a new believer.

When I would miss service Nina would text me and say, "Is everything okay? I noticed you weren't in church." Someone noticed I wasn't there and the next week I'd be sitting in church because Nina was holding me accountable. The friendships I was developing were pushing me closer to God and I was a step closer to the woman I wanted to be as a result of these friendships.

The friends I had lost during this time were a necessary loss for the next step in my life. My old friends and I had all just stayed stagnant together and I hadn't grown much in those years we had spent together. I pray they find their path and happiness. I am no one to judge but I just know that I wasn't happy in those dark places. Do I think my old friends can heal? Of course. Do I think God can help anyone? Yes. Do I think that I should still be in their lives physically? No, but I can pray for them. God only needs a moment to change everything in someone's life. If you must let go of people for God, trust me it will be in your best interest.

Scripture to Meditate

A man of many companions may come to ruin, but there is a friend who sticks closer than a brother.

Proverbs 18:24

He who walks with the wise grows wise, but a companion of fools suffers harm.

Proverbs 13:20

Then Jesus gave the following illustration: "Can one blind person lead another? Won't they both fall into a ditch?

Luke 6:39

Prayer

Lord, help me to let go of friendships that don't serve me. Bring friendships into my life that will help me flourish and grow closer to you. Lord If I have to let go of a friendship please help to fill that void. In Jesus' name, amen.

CHAPTER SIXTEEN

OUR PURPOSE

Our lives here on Earth will be minuscule compared to the eternity we will spend in Heaven if we give our heart to God. Since our time on earth will be only a fraction in time we should focus on cultivating and sharing our God-given gifts while here on earth. There are many stories of those who spent their precious time on earth chasing riches only to find that they're emotionally empty inside. If we live a life that only serves ourselves we'll find ourselves still longing for something greater. I want you to reflect on your gifts for this chapter and think of the way your gifts can serve others and God's kingdom.

Many of us may not be gifted in sports, art, or music but we all have so much to give to the world around us if we look within. We may be good listeners, social servants, or fierce friends. Each of us has something valuable to offer the people around us. A gift like kindness can be shared with anyone and it's still significant to Heaven. I can guarantee that if we use the gifts that God has gifted each of us we'll feel a sense of wholeness and when we go to Heaven we'll hear the Lord say "Well done my good and faithful servant".

If we live frivolously assuming materialism and partying will make our lives richer, we'll find ourselves mistaken. We'll spend our time indulging in destructive habits thinking we are happy yet at night still feel empty, unfulfilled, depressed, and anxious. I thought the purpose of my life was to live to the fullest meaning being in a drunken state several times a week. I spent hours in bars thinking I was living in the prime of my life only to find myself longing for more. Creating a life with God and discovering a purpose that serves others has definitely been the prime of my life.

There are so many ways we can distract ourselves from our purpose so be diligent about how you use your time. I can tell you from experience that substance abuse and partying isn't an effective way to use time. If we 're using those behaviors as a coping mechanism the enemy is using it as a way to keep us distracted from our God-given gifts and keep us away from our purpose. God wants to protect us from our own self-destruction and there are dark spirits that linger waiting for us to be in a weakened spiritual and mental state. The enemy wants to distract us so we don't use our gifts to help others or fulfill God's plan for our life. God's word tells us not to be drunkards, meaning don't be belligerent drunk. Alcohol is a depressant and it does just that, it can lead us into depression if we use it to cope and spend our free time.

In college, I was drinking every weekend and I truly thought I was having a good time and living life to the fullest. I felt I was living the life everyone around me was living. I thought it was fun yet I still felt empty. Those years I spent partying and on drugs, I hadn't really done much with my life. During those moments, I knew I had the capacity to do something more with my life, I just didn't have the discipline to start.

Eventually, I stopped wasting time and I realized I was much more gifted than I had given myself credit for. I also noticed how the enemy kept me distracted while I was partying. I always knew that my purpose was connected to helping people but it wasn't until God pulled me away from that environment that I was able to stand in my purpose. Be willing to let God pull you away from certain environments and friendships. My realization about my gifts came after reading scripture about purpose. I encourage you to read scriptures on purpose and let God speak to you about the next step for your life. Journal everything that comes to mind and list ways that you've been distracted lately.

If God has already given you a dream, career, book, or business idea know that He planted that in your heart. You have the passion and capacity to fulfill those dreams with Him on your side, opening all the right doors. God will give you the strength to shatter glass ceilings and turn to the next woman and say, "I've done it and so can you." For those of us who do have big dreams but are afraid to act because of potential failure, I encourage you to look to God for confidence. Too many of us have let our dreams pass because we're too afraid to fail. The one thing we can count on is that when the Lord gives us an assignment there is no reason to be afraid of failure. With God, anything is possible and He will make a way for us to succeed. The Bible tells us we're all created with a purpose designed by God. God doesn't create us just so we can serve ourselves selfishly and accumulate earthly riches. God is much more interested in your peace, well-being, and love for Him.

Purpose is a life-long process. Each of us can use daily acts of love to fulfill our purpose of loving others. Some of us will be called to do other things in the world but know that our time is so valuable and God gives each of us gifts. A moment without hope for a better future is a moment too long. He creates each of us with a special assignment for our life and no two assignments are the same so we shouldn't compare. Don't let life pass and live with the regret of not stepping out on faith to work with God on your purpose.

God may also have a different purpose for you than you have for yourself. After college, I was confused about my future and during my gap year I was planning to apply to graduate school. Instead, God kept nudging me to write this book that would encourage women and empower them but I kept putting more effort into my graduate school application. When I went to apply for graduate school I found out I was short one course and I wouldn't be able to apply and initially, I was a little upset. Then God kept nudging me again "Work on the book." Sometimes God puts a dream in our hearts that is completely different from our own plan. Be patient with the Lord and be open-minded to what He wants you to do, it may surprise you.

Since I wasn't preoccupied with graduate school, I was able to put all my effort into writing the book and I've poured so much love and time into it. It has taken me so much time to build up the courage to write this book but here I am. Even if you are afraid, apply for the job, turn in the application, work on the project, and start the business. Listen for God, His plan will not fail. There are so many stories in the Bible of people who did what God asked them to do while being afraid. For example, the story of Moses. Moses was afraid of his assignment but God was there to guide him each step of the way and He will be there to guide you.

Moses said, "Please, Lord, send someone else."
Exodus 4:13

Another time God sidetracked me towards His will and away from mine was after I received my degree and I was applying for different jobs that I thought would suit me. I wanted to work with children, a non-profit, or do administrative work for a hospital. I was rejected from a few places and I was upset because I thought I had been called to those places and I thought with a degree I was qualified by the world's standards. During those months while looking for a new job, I was asking God to put me in a place where I could work with women specifically. For a while I was telling my friends, "I'm not worried I know God is going to place me with the right organization." I kept praying to God and asking Him to place me in a position where I could be used by Him. I had always known that my purpose was connected to helping women heal so when I got a call from a women's shelter I thought God had finally answered my prayers only to find out that they had gone with another option. Still, I didn't lose hope I knew I was being called to work with women so after many rejection emails I suddenly got a phone call offering me a job to work at a treatment facility that specifically treated women with eating disorders and co-occurring mental disorders.

God really knows where to place us because I had never been happier at a job. In my heart, I knew I wanted to work with women and specifically that I wanted to work where I could have an impact on their hearts and minds. I also worked with an amazing team and left work feeling fulfilled every day. Had I been hired at any of those other places I might have felt empty and unfulfilled. God is so wonderful and He hears prayers. Have faith that God's plan is always to prosper you and never harm you. Whenever you're disappointed because of a fall back in your career, repeat those words.

God gives us a limited amount of time on earth but can give us eternity in Heaven through salvation. Live a life that Heaven can rejoice about. Be kind to a stranger, pray over friends, and talk to people about God. Not everyone is called to be a preacher but I believe that our lives can be a small reflection of God's love. Some of us are called to be nurses, doctors, lawyers, librarians, volunteers, or authors. If you're rejected from a school or job don't lose hope and stand firm in your faith. Create earthly works that you can be proud of and something that brings glory to God. No matter what we are called to do we can each spread love through small acts of kindness. We each have an assignment in our life and God can use each of us to reflect His love.

Scripture to Meditate

In him we were also chosen, having been predestined according to the plan of him who works out everything in conformity with the purpose of his will

Ephesians 1:11

Do not deceive yourselves. If any of you think you are wise by the standards of this age, you should become "fools" so that you may become wise.

1 Corinthians 3:18

Prayer

Lord, give me the courage to step out on faith and pursue your plan for my life. Lead me to purpose and give me an assignment that fulfills me and honors your kingdom. Give me the courage and confidence to pursue my purpose. Lord banish the spirits of laziness and insecurity. Help me to know that with you I will fulfill my purpose. In Jesus' name, amen.

CHAPTER SEVENTEEN

MAINTAINING A RELATIONSHIP WITH JESUS AND ANGELS

I regularly seek out God anywhere and anytime. As my faith grew I began to seek out God more and in different ways. Sometimes I pray in my room and other times while driving. There are times that I don't ask God for anything during prayer I just have an ongoing conversation about the small details of my day. I've learned that I can approach God as a friend and I can tell Him anything. Prayer time can either be a long-appointed time or a few words to God in the morning.

During my appointed time with Jesus, I read the Bible or pick out specific words that I want to study like peace, letting go, love, or hope.

When I'm in need I boldly come before God and ask for help but I don't seek Him only when I'm in need of something. You can also simply ask God to protect you before leaving the house or thank Him for waking your loved ones in the morning. Seeking out God in small ways throughout the day adds to your relationship with Him. God cares about the details of your life and He wants you to pursue Him.

I listen to worship music while cleaning my apartment or folding laundry. I enjoy spending my time with the Lord. The more I kept looking for healing and answers the deeper I was diving into my relationship with God. The benefit of staying in a consistent relationship with God is that you don't forget that you serve the King above all Kings and no matter how hard things become He will be there for you. Staying in a consistent relationship also keeps you away from unhealthy friendships and relationships because you will be able to detect if they are sent from Him or not. You'll have a spiritual detection system a.k.a. the Holy Spirit that lets you know whether a person should be in your immediate circle or not.

There have been times that I was going through a difficult time and I prayed on my break at work and other times I'd light a candle in my room and pray while on my knees. Every day will be different for you and know that maybe you'll be able to use all these methods to seek God or only one. Building a relationship with God isn't a one size fit all. We all come to Him at different points in our lives and under different circumstances. Still, I want to provide methods that personally helped me strengthen my relationship with God during the beginning of my walk with Him. In the beginning, you may not always have time for a formal appointment with God but try your best to discipline yourself to make time for Him because you will get the answers you're looking for and the opportunity to be in the presence of the Lord and His angels. It feels peaceful being in His presence.

Study yourself very well and figure out a time that works for you. If it's been a busy day just pray while you're on your way somewhere or on your break at work. You may not be able to do some of the things on this list but here are some ideas for you. Also, I want you to remember to be patient with yourself during your walk. I remember when I first started seeking out God I would condemn myself if I didn't have some type of formal appointment with God but know that you can talk to God anywhere and any time of day and for any amount of time and it still matters to God.

Sermons

In the morning if you are getting ready for work or school, take some time to play a YouTube video on your phone. Find a sermon with your favorite pastor and watch the video. I listen to several different pastors during the week, it just depends on who I want to listen to and what message I need to hear for that week. Choose a topic that you feel you need to focus on for your life. After graduation, I was struggling with my purpose so I listened to sermons that focused on purpose and that is how I was led to write this book. Certain pastors reveal key stories in the Bible that focus on areas that you may need more clarity about. The Bible has stories that we can relate to if we're willing to search for them. I personally do my make-up while watching sermons. Whether it's fifteen minutes or an hour, it gives God an opportunity to speak to me and rejuvenate me for the day. I always feel ready to take on the day and I become optimistic about any troubles I'm facing. Also, make sure to have discernment while picking pastors to watch and always ask God about the pastor you're considering following.

Reading the Bible

At first, I didn't understand how to read the Bible or where to start. The first Bible I picked up was the King James Version which I struggled reading. My mom bought me "Battlefield of the Mind Bible: Renew Your Mind Through the Power of God's Word" by Joyce Meyer. This breaks down the Bible and has commentary by the pastor Joyce Meyer. I still have this Bible today, and it is full of post-its, highlighting, and my notes. This Bible helped me break down the word of God.

First, I want to explain how the Bible is structured. There are many books put together that compromise the actual Bible. Some Bibles will give you a summary of each book at the end and others pick a verse and explain it in more detail. When I first started reading the Bible, I looked for the well-known scripture verses and after I started diving more into my journey I sought out scriptures that were not as well-known. I read different chapters and the people in the Bible began to inspire me. I started using the internet to look for all scriptures that applied to my current situation, specifically using keywords. If I was struggling with managing my thoughts, over-thinking, or peace I would go on the internet and search for scripture that had the keyword "peace". After a while of reading all the scriptures that had the word peace, I would feel an overwhelming sense of peace about my current situation. Later in the day if I still struggled with overthinking and anxiety, I would say out loud some of the scriptures I had read earlier. Reading the Bible gave me the tools I needed to avoid the enemy's attacks on my mind throughout the day and it taught me to put my faith in God as opposed to being overwhelmed by spiritual attacks. Saying the scripture out loud reminded me that I was depending on God to come and help me with peace and that He would not leave me. God is bigger than your worries, fears, and anything against you.

Podcasts

I use podcasts while driving, at the gym and while I clean my apartment. Some of my favorite pastors have podcasts. The podcasts vary in length and style. If I can't sit and watch a video, I just use my earphones to listen to a podcast led by my favorite pastors. This helps me renew for my day if I do it right in the morning even if it's just for 15 minutes.

Favorite authors

As I started to listen to different pastors, I found that many of them have written books. Since I enjoyed many of their sermons and style of teaching, I would order many of their books. Reading about their testimony and some of the trials they overcame with God reassured me that others have gone through similar trials. Their testimonies also taught me many things about faith. Sometimes I can't read every day so I read when I can. I try to get a chapter done each week depending on how busy my week is.

Journal

Keeping a journal during your journey is key to realizing how much you're growing. Reading my old journals allowed me to see all the things that I was worried about that I probably didn't need to worry about because God was going to take care of it. It also showed me the times I was desperate for God and the times I was just joyful. I make sure to write all the time. I write about my joy just as much as I write about my sorrow. It shows me the times the Lord answered my prayers and the different ways He answered. Sometimes He answered my prayer right away and other times He didn't answer immediately. Having a journal has taught me that all my seasons were necessary and God is molding me continuously. I recommend keeping a journal and when you feel like God isn't working in your life you can see all the ways He has.

Finding a Church

For a while I thought pursuing God was great alone until I ran into a difficult time. I didn't want to ask for advice from my old friends because they weren't on the same journey as me. I needed godly people that could offer me godly perspective and the place where I could meet godly people was at church. I started to use the church as a charging station for myself. I would go Sunday so I could be renewed for the new week. I noticed when I stopped going to church on Sundays, I was giving the enemy an opportunity to attack my mind and he did. It says in the Bible the devil is looking for an opportunity to attack and when we're not paying attention to our prayer life that is the perfect opportunity because we're not close to God. All of sudden doubt, fear, and anxiety creeps in. I recommend finding a church you can go to and finding a community that can support and keep you accountable during your journey.

While deciding to stay at a church make sure to evaluate the pastor. I needed a pastor who I could trust to deliver the word of God and live by the words preached on Sunday morning. Pastors Julio and Kim Mancia were incredibly instrumental in my journey and truly authentic people. They were always transparent and honest at church which I valued and respected. They had a way of making people feel loved and welcomed despite their flaws. They are so loved and appreciated by many people. Pastors will not always tell you what you'd like to hear, that's not their job. Their job is to lead people to God and lovingly correct people in the church according to God's standards. Have discernment and pay attention to your spiritual compass (The Holy Spirit) and if something feels off with a church or pastor then maybe that's not the church for you and try somewhere else. But if you get upset that the pastor is telling people not to sin, that's their job as a pastor.

When I first started my journey, I didn't go to church every Sunday and sometimes I would miss church for one or two weeks. Sometimes this will happen when you start your journey with God. As I developed my faith I started to go to church more often because I realized I was the one benefiting from diving deeper with God. I no longer went out of obligation or because I thought I was building up "Heaven points". God knows our hearts and we should go to church because we honor and love Him. If God calls you to go to church, go to church. Like I've mentioned before, everyone's journey will look different and happens at different times.

Serving

I never thought I'd be good with children. I grew up an only child and didn't spend much time with other children in my neighborhood, my cousins came to visit occasionally, but I spent much of the time with my grandmother. So, when the church announced that it needed help in the children's ministry, I didn't raise my hand. After a few days my heart felt compelled to join the children's ministry. The children's ministry is a childcare where kids learn about Jesus. Each Sunday there is a specific lesson plan taught for specific age groups.

I started as a teacher's aide for the ages 3-5 class and my first day I absolutely loved it. There was something so fulfilling about teaching the word of Jesus to kids. Their answer for everything was "Jesus loves us" and it reminded me of the childlike faith we're supposed to have as adults. Not everyone will be called to be in the children's ministry but there are different areas of the church that do need help and at some point, you will be called to serve in some way. When I serve, I always remember that I'm serving the Lord in my service to the church, so I do it with a cheerful heart and I'm so honored to serve God's children.

LOVE

Love is the most important. How we love is how we bridge the gap between us and God. Once we heal from our brokenness there is room to love ourselves, God, and others. Love isn't always romantic. I've learned to love strangers when no one is watching. I remember this one time I met a homeless man who left his mark on my heart. He was in front of a store and asked me for a favor as I was walking into the store. When I was struggling financially, I gave what I could to others because in the Bible it says what you've done for a stranger surely, you've done for Jesus.

I was in a hurry and this man asked me to get him a gift card to Subway since I was walking into the store. I was running late and there was traffic but something told me to buy this man the gift card and so I did. When I came back out, I asked him if I could pray for him and he said yes. To my surprise, he asked if he could pray for me. After I finished uttering the last words of my prayer, this man began to pray, "Lord, thank you for this woman because any other woman as beautiful as her would have just ignored me. I pray that you are a light in her life. I pray she knows that she is worthy. I pray for protection over her." I thought I was a blessing to him but after his prayer, I realized I was the one deeply blessed to have encountered him.

I instantly felt my heart soften and I realized how powerful his prayer was. I still think of that moment and I know God was there in that moment between both of us. He heard His children covering each other in love and prayer.

Again, truly I tell you that if two of you on earth agree about anything they ask for, it will be done for them by my Father in Heaven. For where two or three gather in my name, there am I with them

Matthew 18:19-20

I now understand the power people possess while praying over each other. There are different ways to demonstrate love. We can pray over each other or encourage each other. Love is so powerful. As I developed my relationship with God my capacity to love grew, and my love continues to grow. Your love will grow too and you will not fear loving because you'll know that God loves you fiercely and restores your love every minute.

Angels

Another beautiful asset I added to my spiritual life was angels. I called upon angels to guide and protect me, especially the archangel Michael. During a very difficult time, I was praying fervently for the archangel Michael. I felt very broken and I asked Archangel Michael to help protect me from any spirits trying to affect my mind. The next morning, I felt lighter as if I was protected and I made it a regular practice to seek out angels for help as well as Jesus Christ and the Holy Spirit. I want to encourage you to ask your own personal guardian angel for help and archangels for guidance during your spiritual journey and know that you have divine beings that want to help you heal and move forward.

Nature

I also changed my environment while praying. Sometimes I would drive to a garden or local park and read the Bible. I would silence my phone so I could be in touch with nature and God and just lay in the grass. I'd make sure to take a snack, water, and I just sat in the presence of God. I wasn't distracted by phone calls, emails, or messages. I was able to write in my prayer journal and really listen for God and let Him guide the next steps of my life. Our lives are so fast paced that we miss the beautiful parts of it. The smile of a loved one, the laughter of a child, the beautiful trees, flowers, and the environment God has created. Most of the time we're in traffic or in our own minds worried about the next step in life but if we sit with God we won't have to worry about the next step, He will give us clear guidance. Take a moment to step away from the busyness of everyday life and enjoy God outdoors. It will give you a moment of stillness and peace.

Travel

I also would like to encourage you to make time to travel. I love to feel the beauty that traveling has to offer. I enjoy experiencing God's people in other parts of the world. If you can I would encourage you to save money and take a trip. Life is too short, and trips can help us disconnect from the routine of everyday life and soak in the beautiful places God has created around the world. Every time I'm on vacation I make sure to pack my Bible and my prayer journal. In my journal, I thank God for the opportunity to travel and express how grateful I am for Him.

Scripture to Meditate

Your word is a lamp to my feet and a light to my path
Psalm 119:105

All Scripture is God-breathed and is useful for teaching, rebuking, correcting and training in righteousness,
2 Timothy 3:16

Don't be afraid, for I am with you. Don't be discouraged, for I am your God. I will strengthen you and I will help you. I will hold you up with my victorious right hand.
Isaiah 41:10

For the word of God is alive and active. Sharper than any double-edged sword, it penetrates even to dividing soul and spirit, joints and marrow; it judges the thoughts and attitudes of the heart.
Hebrews 4:12

CHAPTER EIGHTEEN

STORMS WILL COME

Starting a relationship with Jesus doesn't mean that obstacles and challenges will never come into your life again. I'd be lying if I said you could get through life without another obstacle but maintaining a consistent relationship with Jesus will mean you never have to go through storms alone. The Creator of the universe is with us even in the darkest moments of our lives. Walking with God during storms taught me that pain eventually subsides. Whether the pain comes from a decision we make or something that was completely out of our control, we can deal with it the same way— press into God. The Lord is our greatest comforter and He bears the weight of our pain if we ask Him.

We can seek Him for emotional health, physical health, and mental health. The best part about seeking God our comforter is that we can cry and admit how desperate we are without our ego in the way. In life, we will encounter minor inconveniences like a flat tire or bigger issues like the death of a loved one. In the moments of minor inconveniences, they may feel like a huge storm but even in those small inconvenient moments, we can be sure that God is still with us. More pressing issues like loss, death, heartbreak, and abandonment will come up throughout our life. We can't go through life thinking storms will never come but we can be better prepared for those storms by maintaining our walk with Jesus. Those severe issues do not mean that God does not love you or that He has forgotten you.

In the book of Job, we see a man that loses everything but still holds on to God. He loses his home, his family, his health, yet he still had faith that the Lord was on his side despite his unfortunate circumstances. We are no different, God loves us even through the darkest moments of our life.

A few months ago I got into an accident that totaled my car and the following week I lost my phone which had all my passwords to my email accounts. The morning of the accident I had spent an hour with God telling Him how grateful I was for everything He had done for me. My life felt so beautiful and I was experiencing joy all the time.

Around the same time of the accident, I began to worry about my health, my grandparents, and managing work. I thought to myself "God are you upset with me?" The insurance was not going to cover the damages and I was really upset about it for weeks. I had to borrow my mom's car to get to work and it felt like God was just not on my side. After some time I just accepted things and kept praying to God to carry my burdens.

At some point, the Holy Spirit reminded me that I wasn't in a relationship with God for tangible things and He showed me how quickly tangible things can be taken from us. It was a valuable lesson and an important learning experience. I finally learned that the treasures here on Earth are worthless compared to treasures God has to offer. A few months later I was able to put a down payment for a new car and luckily the phone store mentioned I was due for an upgrade so everything worked out. My health soon restored once I could say "Lord, I don't understand but I'm going to have a cheerful heart even though it's hard to accept my circumstances."

Another ongoing storm in my life is my family. There is usually turmoil amongst my family and it can be stressful wanting everyone to get along. This experience has taught me to cast my care onto the Lord and know my own personal limitations. I thought I had control over everything became very stressful. Even a phone call became draining for me spiritually until I learned to cast it unto the Lord. After a phone call I would say, "Lord this out of my control, I wish I could solve all their problems because I love them but I can't."

We can't always solve everything, but we can cast our worry upon the Lord, entrusting our troubles to Him. God is not like humans whom we have to second guess. He will take care of things and He handles business on His time, not ours. Sometimes it will take time for God to come through and other times He will respond immediately, but it doesn't mean He doesn't care if He takes a little longer. Don't lose hope and remember the God we serve will not let you down. Don't let the enemy steal your faith by listening to whispers from him saying that "God doesn't care or He's taking too long". Immediately cast those thoughts away and respond "My God is bigger than you and I trust Him and His timing."

Doubt

Doubt steals more dreams than anything else. We doubt our capacity to carry out our dreams. We start a project but never finish. We blame it on the fact that we're too busy but the truth is that we can't grapple with the idea of failure. While I was writing this book I had moments of doubt but I remembered God gave me this assignment to carry out. It helps if we remember that God has an assignment on our lives. Someone out there is waiting for you to be obedient to God. People are waiting to see a woman start a successful business, write the book, create the program, finish the creative project. You can break glass ceilings with God. You can achieve anything with God's favor and Heaven on your side. It's up to you to believe in yourself enough to start.

During college, I struggled with self-doubt. I was Latina and I was raised in the San Fernando Valley. No one in my family had graduated from college and some of my relatives struggled with addiction. I didn't think I would get accepted into college let alone finish with a bachelor's in science but here I am. The first in my family to receive a bachelor's degree and now the first to be an author. Doubt is a liar and when we entertain feelings of doubt we keep ourselves small. The devil rejoices when you sulk in self-doubt and low confidence.

Take a leap of faith and remember with God there is no limit to things you can accomplish. Moments when it is hard to believe in yourself remember the God you serve and the assignment He has placed on your life. When the enemy pushes you to doubt your beauty, intelligence, or confidence reclaim authority over your mind and learn to interrupt those destructive thoughts. When you hear any of these thoughts, cast them down.

- "You won't be accepted to the school."
- "People will never read the book."
- "You're just like your mother/father."
- "No one has done it before."
- "You aren't good enough."
- "You aren't pretty enough."
- "You aren't smart enough."

After dismissing the negative thoughts begin to reframe your thoughts with Godly statements.

- "I will get into the school with God's help."
- "I have some valuable insight to offer readers."
- "I was created by God and He is molding me into a better woman."
- "I will be the first to branch out with God's help."
- "I'm good enough because God created me."
- "I'm beautiful because God created me."
- "I'm intelligent because I seek God for wisdom."

When a negative thought begins to flow through your mind just start to speak aloud "That isn't true." If you can't believe in yourself, believe in God. He'll open doors for you if you just have the faith to take one step at a time.

Scripture to Meditate

I have said these things to you, that in me you may have peace. In the world, you will have tribulation. But take heart; I have overcome the world.
John 16:33

Be strong and courageous. Do not be afraid; Do not be discouraged, for the Lord your God will be with you wherever you go.
Joshua 1:9

Don't be afraid, for I am with you. Don't be discouraged, for I am your God. I will strengthen you and I will help you. I will hold you up with my victorious right hand.
Isaiah 41:10

For his anger lasts only a moment, but his favor lasts a lifetime; weeping may stay for the night, but rejoicing comes in the morning.
Psalm 30:5

We are afflicted in every way, but not crushed; perplexed, but not driven to despair; persecuted, but not forsaken; struck down, but not destroyed
2 Corinthians 4:8-9

But now thus says the Lord, he who created you, O Jacob, he who formed you, O Israel: "Fear not, for I have redeemed you; I have called you by name, you are mine. When you pass through the waters, I will be with you; and through the rivers, they shall not overwhelm you; when you walk through fire you shall not be burned, and the flame shall not consume you.

Isaiah 43:1-2

Prayer

Lord, give me the wisdom to seek you during this difficult time. Although difficult obstacles may come, I know you'll never abandon me. When things become difficult help me to press into you. In Jesus' name, amen.

CHAPTER NINETEEN

HEALING HEART

This book is just one of the steps in your journey but you get to continue a relationship with God the rest of your life should you choose. I don't promise that trials and tests won't come throughout your journey because they will. We can't avoid the troubles of life but we can walk through life with God. He carries our current troubles and He can heal our past.

I've explained the different ways you can seek out God and I hope you can find a practice that brings you closer to God. When I first started my relationship, I thought I had to be perfect to come to God and I'd condemn myself for falling short because I kept making mistakes. I would stop reading the Bible, miss church, or hurt someone's feelings and feel discouraged about my walk with Jesus. Just because you make a mistake doesn't mean you have to give up entirely or feel that you are inadequate. God forgives us. I want to normalize that mistakes will happen, but God will forgive you. He understands your journey so be patient with yourself and when you make a mistake, get up, and dust yourself off and continue to follow God. When you feel like returning to your past or old ways of thinking remember that you've outgrown that version of yourself then keep moving, keep growing. Even when it's hard and it hurts emotionally move forward toward God and you will come out on the other side of the storm. Even when it feels like God isn't listening, He is. He hears every prayer, petition, and cry.

You are loved unconditionally by God and He wants to fill your life with joy and surround you with love. All it takes is having the courage to trust God to remove the friendships and relationships that no longer suit you and know that what is coming is much better than what you've lost. Many people mistakenly think a life with God means no fun but what it actually means is a life filled with peace and love. We can seek God wherever we are in life and we don't have to be perfect to start a relationship with Him.

I pray that you are healed from any heartbreak and you realize that you are a phenomenal woman created by God. I pray you never settle for less than you deserve. I pray that you let go of the disappointments of those who have hurt you. I pray that you have the courage to trust that you are loved by a loving and powerful God. I pray healing and restoration over your heart and mind. I pray that you step into the woman that God called you to be and I pray that you are fearless when it comes to your purpose. I pray that if you're ever lost that you know God will go into the darkness to bring you back into His light again.

For it is by grace you have been saved, through faith—and this is not from yourselves, it is the gift of God— not by works, so that no one can boast.

Ephesians 2:8-9

Love,

Marissa Ortiz-Cortez

@_marisscortez

Made in the USA
Monee, IL
20 June 2023

36448426R00103